I0159958

The Art of Knowing

Expositions on Free Will and Selected Essays

Revised and Expanded Edition

CHRISTOPHER M. LANGAN

The Art of Knowing

Expositions on Free Will
and Selected Essays

Revised and Expanded Edition

Mega Foundation Press

Copyright © 1998–2021 by Christopher M. Langan

All rights reserved. No part of this publication may be reproduced or transmitted, in any form or by any means, electronic, mechanical, photocopying, recorded, or otherwise, without the prior permission of Christopher Michael Langan. It is illegal to copy this book, post it to a website, or distribute it by any other means without permission. Reprinted with permission of the author, August 2021. Mega Foundation Press is a trademark of the Mega Foundation, Inc.

Revised and Expanded
Paperback Edition

Published by
Mega Foundation Press
Princeton, MO

info@megapress.org

Typeset in Merriweather
by Michał Szczęsny

www.ctmu.org

www.patreon.com/CTMU

Langan, C. M. (Christopher Michael)

The Art of Knowing:
Expositions on Free Will and Selected Essays
Revised and Expanded Edition

1. Metaphysics 2. General Knowledge

ISBN 978-0-9719162-4-1

CONTENTS

Publisher's Note vii

PART I

So You Want to Be a Millionaire?
All It Will Cost You Is Your Freedom 1

The Buck Starts Here:
Another Disquisition on Free Will 11

A Free Will Cyber-Synthesis 21

Solutions for the Problems of Free Will,
Good and Evil, Consciousness and God 31

PART II

On the Perils of Metaphysical
Skysurfing Without a Parachute 45

A *Very* Brief History of Time 53

Which Came First? 61

Of Trees, Quads and God 69

The Pros and Cons of "Machine Intelligence" 79

In Ethics, Not Everything is Relative 87

Millennium Mouse: An Ecological Parable 95

PART III

IQ, IEQ and Intelligence 99

On High-Ceiling Intelligence Tests 103

On Absolute Truth and Knowledge 109

The Theory of Theories 121

On Ayn Rand's Philosophy 135

REFERENCES 141

Publisher's Note

Although best known as the creator of the Cognitive-Theoretic Model of the Universe, Christopher Michael Langan has been publishing philosophical essays on a wide variety of topics for more than 40 years. While reflecting his diverse interests, these essays tend to gravitate toward a recurrent theme: the intimate, multifaceted connection between physical reality and human cognitive processes. This is a revised and expanded edition of the popular 2002 collection of the same name.

Special thanks to the members of the CTMU Media Workshop who help preserve and present Chris Langan's work and ideas.

PART I

So You Want to Be a Millionaire?
All It Will Cost You Is Your Freedom

Imagine that you snagged some tickets from a buddy at NBC and are now a lucky member of the studio audience on the celebrated *Tonight Show*. The Tonight Show Band fires up and Jay Leno emerges.

"Thank you ... thank you!" says Big Jay through the applause.

"I'm proud to announce that we have some very interesting guests on the show tonight. In fact, one of them is known for seemingly inhuman powers of prediction ... powers that he will demonstrate on a member of this very audience!" (Kevin Eubanks spookily simulates a theremin on his electric guitar.)

"And thanks to the cooperation of my friend Regis Philbin, that lucky audience member will have the chance to walk away with *one million dollars!*" (You and I both know that a Leno–Philbin collaboration would cross the Major Network Divide and is thus forbidden. So just consider it a suspension-of-disbelief thing.)

Jay does his monologue, trots out his first couple of guests. Finally, the magic moment arrives.

"And now the event you've all been waiting for," crows Jay. "It is my pleasure to introduce a veritable modern-day Nostradamus, the most amazing mentalist in history, Sir Damon Nukem!"

Nukem, tall of stature and angelic of countenance, emerges to thunderous applause. Everyone in the audience, including you, already knows exactly who he is; a regular in the *National Enquirer*, he's reputed to be an alien, to wear contact lenses that conceal yellow irises with vertical pupils, and even to have a couple of goatish horns under his immaculately coiffed hair. (Fortunately, you're not the kind of person who believes everything you read.) One thing you know for sure, however, is that he's the world's foremost mentalist, having correctly predicted the behavior of thousands of people in hundreds of different contexts under a wide variety of conditions. He has never failed . . . not once.

In Nukem's most notorious routine, he offers a randomly chosen contestant a choice between one or both of two boxes, one of which (Box A) is transparent and contains a thousand dollars, and one of which (Box B) is opaque and contains either a million dollars or nothing at all. That is, the contestant is allowed two possible choices: (1) to take just the opaque box B, or (2) to take both boxes (A and B). Here's the catch: a neutral referee, usually either professional debunker James Randi or an equally curmudgeonly associate of the *Skeptical Enquirer*, holds a single well-sealed envelope containing a single slip of paper on which Nukem has written a prediction regarding the contestant's choice. If the slip says "B", then Box B contains a million dollars; if the slip says "A and B", then Box B contains nothing. In other words, if Nukem has predicted that the contestant will leave the thousand on the table, then there is $1,001,000 on the table; if Nukem has predicted that the contestant will grab the "extra" thousand, then what you see is exactly what you get, and there is nothing more on the table than the price of a good office chair.

Common sense tells you that since the prediction is already in the sealed envelope at the moment the contestant makes his or her choice, he or she can lose nothing by taking both boxes and grabbing the extra thousand. No disrespect to Nukem – he does, after all, seem to be on a world-class lucky streak when it comes to prognostication – but what's done is done, and things will unfold according to the Grand Plan regardless of what anybody thinks. Even if Nukem somehow scans the brain or reads the mind of the contestant before making his prediction, and even if this causes a million dollars to be placed in Box B, there is obviously nothing stopping the contestant from changing his mind at the last minute and snagging that extra thousand. After all, that's what free will is all about. And an extra grand could be the difference between banking that million at the autoteller in Hampton Bays, and personally depositing it in a special account in the Bahamas during a cut-rate Princess Cruise with the Significant Other!

But the thing is, the prediction in the envelope always turns out to be correct, and no matter how hard Randi and his buddies have tried to catch Nukem in a mistake or a deception, the mentalist always comes up squeaky clean. Somehow, Nukem knows exactly how much confidence the contestant has in his abilities. Those who believe that he has predicted correctly and choose accordingly are always rewarded with a seven-figure retirement fund; those who think they can "pull a fast one" at the eleventh hour and belie his prediction are doomed to kick their own cans forever after for throwing away a certified ticket to Easy Street, the additional $999,000 they'd have won had they merely given predictive credit where credit was due. Furthermore, Nukem never seems to force the issue; when questioned, all of the contestants report that their choices were made "freely".

Lost in your reverie, you realize that someone with a distinctive nasal tenor is speaking into your ear. Fearing the worst, you look up just in time to see a gigantic boulder crashing down on you from above! Then you see what it really is: The Chin. It positively blocks the sky.

"Excuse me . . . are we boring you here?"

"Er, not at all," you quickly respond.

Everybody laughs at you.

"I'm very happy to hear that," says Leno. "Because we were just about to call security!"

Everybody laughs at you again. You feel pathetic.

"Anyway, I'm pleased to inform you that you've been chosen as the lucky contestant who will have a chance to win One Million Dollars!"

He sticks the mike under your nose.

"Uh, er ... sure," you say, nodding.

"OK then," says Leno as he takes you by the elbow. "Let's go!"

Before you know it, you're up on the *Tonight Show* stage. The lights are blinding. With a flourish, Nukem draws a curtain, and there they sit: two boxes on a table. As expected, one of them is transparent and contains ten crisp $100 bills; the other is larger and opaque. The audience falls silent as Newcomb begins to speak, his voice at once hypnotic and resonant. Your ears buzz as he recites a game description that sounds like a magician's incantation. Finally, he finishes, gestures dramatically towards the table, and folds his arms across his chest. The fateful juncture has arrived: you must choose! Will it be the opaque box, or will it be both boxes? Will you embrace Nukem's predictive infallibility and place all your faith in his ability to predict your behavior, or will you use this moment in the spotlight to strike a blow for common sense, freedom of choice, and an extra G in your checking account?

Well – what'll it be?

Alright, alright, let's stop the clock and think about this for a minute. If the opaque box contains the million dollars, taking just that box will earn you a cool million. But why would you do that, when you could easily grab the transparent box as well and make an additional grand? After all, the contents of the opaque box won't suddenly change simply because you decide to take the other one too. This whole setup has been checked out by Randi and his antiparanormal goon squad, and they've made sure that the contents of the boxes are as safe and unchanging as the laws of physics can make them. On the other hand, if the opaque box is empty, then that thousand dollars in the transparent box is your only chance to walk away with anything at all! When you think about it in these terms, it really looks as though the issue is cut and dried. You might as well cover all bets and take both boxes.

But as long as we've already got a suspension of disbelief going, that's not the only way to look at it. Nukem has quite a track record, and it hardly seems rational to ignore it. The fact that he has played this game a thousand times and been right a thousand times – well, the odds against that are 2 to the thousandth power to one, and thus way beyond astronomical. This alone would seem to suggest that the laws of physics may not be everything they're cracked up to be. Doesn't particle physics recognize time as flowing in both directions? Nukem is either passively reading the future without affecting it, or actively controlling the thought and behavior of his contestants in such a way that they cannot directly detect his influence. In any case, statistical induction would seem to indicate that the contestant's chance of beating the renowned mentalist at his own game are around one half to the thousandth power, as close to nothing as one can get without falling through the zero. You might as well bet against death, taxes and $1 + 1 = 2$!

Then again, there are a couple of philosophical kinks in the wire. The first one, *Goodman's Grue*, is about the limitations of induction. Suppose you have two hypotheses, namely "emeralds are green", and "emeralds are green and will so remain until New Year's Day 2050, at which point they will all turn blue." (This can also be expressed by saying that "emeralds are grue", where "grue" is defined as "green until 2050 and blue thereafter".) Statistically, both of these hypotheses are equally confirmed by current observations. This implies that Nukem's past successes can also be regarded as confirming two hypotheses, namely "Nukem is able to predict the future" and "Nukem was able to predict the future up to the last contest, but not thereafter." With loopholes like that, arguments from induction can be hard to trust.

On the other hand, laws of physics are themselves discovered by induction. This suggests that all of the observations and experiments confirming the currently accepted laws of physics also support the following hypothesis: "The currently-known laws of physics hold perfectly well until Damon Nukem decides to predict the future, at which point they bend subtly to his will." This, of course, raises an important question: in what kind of reality could a prognosticator like Nukem bend the laws of physics with the power of his will, yet remain undetected? Even if his powers are entirely passive, even if he only "watches" the future without ever taking a hand in it, how can he transcend the flow of time? Where time is understood to progress steadily from past to future, how can his mind leapfrog into the future and back again? How can information go from future to past?

Suddenly you remember a hit movie called *The Matrix*. What if the world is a kind of digital simulation running on a powerful computer and displayed on a vast quantum-pixelated 3D monitor? What if "people" are just software homunculi who consider themselves sentient, but cannot detect the higher level of reality containing the computer and its programmer? Perhaps the programmer of such a simulation could influence the behavior of these homunculi without being detected. In fact, maybe he could freeze the action, fast-forward the program, gather information on future events, back the program up to the "present moment" and resume the simulation precisely where it left off so that nobody inside would ever know. What if Nukem has a direct line to the Great Programmer in the sky, or maybe His competition down below? Where would the laws of physics, including the flow of time, be then?

Breaking surface from your deep concentration, you look around the studio. The audience is murmuring and shifting in their seats. Nukem, looking as much as possible like the Antichrist, is glaring at you with his arms still folded. Leno is looking conspicuously at his wristwatch and making silly faces in your direction. Obviously, your time is up. Your heart pounding in your chest, you make your choice and announce it. And when the opaque box is opened . . .

Nukem the Magnificent is right again!

Now, among the questions you're probably asking are these: What is this story really about? Why is this guy writing about it? Where did it originally come from, and when? And how is anybody supposed to make sense of it, when it's obviously crazy? The answers, in order: This story is about free will.

6

I'm writing about free will because I find the topic very interesting (as should you). The basic story, minus a few stylistic and atmospheric touches of my own, originally came from a physicist named William Newcomb and was popularized by the Harvard philosopher Robert Nozick circa 1969. (As we will see, it is no accident that the story originally came from a physicist.) And if you think it's crazy, it's not because you can *prove* it's crazy, but only because you *assume* it's crazy. For all you really know, it could actually happen.

In case you're wondering why I say that you "should be" interested in free will, I'll risk belaboring the obvious and point out that the free will question ranks right up there with "Is there a God?" and "What is the meaning of life?" among philosophical riddles. Moreover, although philosophers have long treated free will as an open question, more practical minds long ago jumped the gun on their lofty discourse and adopted free will as a foregone conclusion. Most of us mirror their position: because we feel as though we are exercising free will in order to make decisions and perform voluntary actions, we take its existence for granted. Our social, political and religious structures, as well as our ideas about human dignity, human rights, civil liberties, moral responsibility, crime and punishment, and good and evil are already heavily invested in the concept ... heavily enough that if the existence of free will were ever disproved, it would literally destroy everything we believe about ourselves and the world we inhabit.

The above scenario, along with the question of how the contestant should choose, is found in the literature under the names "Newcomb's Problem" and "Newcomb's Paradox". Although one might be tempted to assume that they mean the same thing, there is a subtle difference between the "problem" and the "paradox". In order to solve Newcomb's Problem, one must explain how the contestant should choose and why.

Unfortunately, there are two possible ways to do this, and it is extremely difficult to say which one of them is right. In fact, it's so difficult that they are regarded as having equal claim on correctness. And that's where Newcomb's Paradox enters the picture: two "equally correct solutions" that contradict each other add up to a paradox, plain and simple. To resolve the paradox, one must do one of three things:

1. Decide the issue, showing why one solution is correct (and the other incorrect).

2. Describe a framework into which both solutions fit under different circumstances.

3. Prove the scenario unreal and the question meaningless.

How might one achieve a resolution of Newcomb's paradox? First, one would need to know more about the solutions of the problem on which it centers. The first, "take both boxes", is called the *dominance* solution. The second, "take only the opaque box", is called the *expected utility* solution. The dominance solution is supported by the idea that since time runs in only one direction, the player can lose nothing by taking the extra thousand dollars in the transparent box; the million is either in the opaque box or it is not, and this fact is not subject to last-minute change. The expected utility solution, on the other hand, is a straightforward calculation of mathematical expectation based on statistical induction from Nukem's long and unbroken string of successful predictions. One simply constructs a payoff matrix for the game defined by the Newcomb scenario, computes the expected value of each possible move, and chooses the move with the highest value.

So much for the current philosophical impasse regarding Newcomb's paradox. In order to progress beyond this point, we need to avail ourselves of a branch of mathematical logic called *model theory*. According to model theory, using a theory to correctly describe some part of the world is logically equivalent to specifying a valid *interpretation* of that theory, which means specifying a *model* of the theory. In this case, the theories are the rationales used to justify the solutions, and the models of those theories are their (superficially) valid interpretations in the real world ... assuming, of course, that the Newcomb scenario is possible in the real world, which is a bit of a stretch (in this context, "valid" means only "not yet invalidated"). The key ingredient of the dominance model is a one-way arrow of time, while the key ingredient of the expected utility model is a natural induction principle. While neither of these ingredients is yet a well-understood feature of reality, neither has yet been disproved. But the fact remains that they have sharply conflicting implications in the Newcomb scenario, and therein resides the paradox.

That Newcomb's Paradox can be reduced to conflicting elements in a hypothetical configuration of physical reality suggests that its proper resolution requires a theory and model of reality in which the relationship between these elements can be meaningfully evaluated. In other words, we need a theory of reality in which we can explore the nature of time in an inductive context. This is why, several paragraphs ago, I called it "no accident" that the paradox was originally cooked up by a physicist; physicists are among those most concerned with the nature of time and the inductive derivation of functional theories of reality. Insofar as weird or improbable scenarios have held the keys to new insight many times in the history of science, the far-out nature of the paradox is beside the point. Where the stakes include a better understanding of time, induction and free will, even a scenario as unlikely as Newcomb's is worth a gander.

The Buck Starts Here:
Another Disquisition on Free Will

In the previous essay we talked about free will, and I asked you to pretend that you were playing an imaginary game taken from the hypothetical philosophical scenario called "Newcomb's Paradox". In this essay, we're still talking about free will. But this time, I'm asking you to imagine that you're part of a scientific experiment.

You're seated at a table with electrodes glued to your head. Across from you sits a man in a white lab coat with a clipboard and a stopwatch. There's a camera on the ceiling; mounted on the wall in front of you is some kind of fancy clock with a bright circle of light revolving rapidly around its face where a second hand should be. The man carefully explains what he wants you to do.

"Over the next few minutes, you will be expected to make spontaneous, freely-initiated movements of your right hand. The movements should consist of simple flexions of your right wrist. Any time you want to move your hand, you can and should do so of your own free will. All you have to do is keep your eye on the clock and report the position of the circle at the precise moment you decide to act."

You agree.

"Then let's begin," says the man.

Keeping your eye on the revolving circle, you mentally command your hand to move and note the position of the circle at the instant you make your decision. You report the circle's position: halfway between 9 and 10 o'clock. The man marks this down. You continue. Again and again you move your hand, each time reporting the position of the circle at the exact moment you decide to do so; each time, the man marks it down on his clipboard. Finally, he indicates that he is satisfied.

"Very good," he tells you. "That will suffice. In the name of science, we thank you."

"My pleasure," you say, getting up and unceremoniously unpeeling the electrodes from your scalp. "I hope this helps clarify what goes on in the human brain after a person decides to commit a voluntary act!"

"I'm certain your data will be of great help," says the man. "But since you've been so kind as to participate in the experiment, let me clarify one little detail for you. This experiment was not about what went on in your brain *after* you decided to act. Everything of interest, including the initial electrical brain potential precipitating each of your actions, occurred considerably *before* you consciously decided to act."

With a slight smirk, the scientist turns and walks out of the room.

Wait a minute here. The initial electrical brain potential precipitating each of your actions occurred *before* you decided to act? But then how could you have been acting of your own free will? What was that white-smocked lab geek talking about? Who did he think he was, amusing himself at the expense of an experimental subject – Doctor Giggles? What were they pumping through those electrodes? And who cares about a far-fetched hypothetical experiment like this one anyway?

Well, maybe not so hypothetical. In 1983, an experiment just like this one was performed at the Neurological Institute at San Francisco's Mount Zion Hospital and Medical Center, and reported in the journal *Brain* in a paper entitled "Time of Conscious Intention to Act in Relation to Onset of Cerebral Activity (Readiness-Potential)" by Libet, Gleason, Wright and Pearl. The paper reported that after subjects were invited to make freely-timed voluntary movements of their right hands, an electrical brain wave called the *Bereitschaftspotential* ("readiness-potential") appeared over the motor areas of their left cerebral hemispheres some 500 to 800 milliseconds (0.5–0.8 seconds) before they were aware of intending to act, with muscular electrical activity not appearing until its near-completion another 0.2 seconds later. On the basis of these data, the experimenters concluded that voluntary neural activity appears to be preceded by physiological neural activity, and that even though awareness of intent comes almost a second after the onset of the neural activity in question, it is interpreted by the subject as having come "first". In other words, a voluntary act may begin well in advance of the conscious intent to perform it, but the subject interprets things the other way around.

Where does this leave free will? Right about where causality would be if it were ever found that what we think are "causes" actually occur *after* their "effects": in the OUT basket. Could we really be so clueless that what we call our "intentions" are just delusions that occur only after our actions are first initiated by our subconscious minds, perhaps under the rigid guidance of deterministic mechanisms in light of which we amount to little more than self-deluding automata? What could possibly be going on here?

Let's begin by taking a look at bodily movements in general. A *reflex* is an automatic muscular reaction that does not directly involve the brain. Because reflexes have a protective function, speed is of the essence, and the resulting movements are general enough that no conscious action is required. An example is the patellar reflex, the familiar medical "knee-jerk test" in which the tendon just below the kneecap is tapped with a rubber hammer. In a healthy patient, this causes a quick, unintended outward jerk of the lower leg. Why? The tap of the hammer triggers sensory nerve cells that send a message to the spinal cord.

Ordinarily, sensory stimuli travel up the spinal cord to the brain for conscious processing, but not in this case. Instead, the spinal cord responds directly to motor neurons in the muscle, causing the muscle to contract and the lower leg to kick out. Although the brain seems to exercise a general one-way "gating effect" influencing reflexes throughout the body, the sense-response loop or "reflex arc" never gets far

13

enough up the spinal cord for brain-based conscious volition to specifically intervene. A particular reflex can be surprising to one experiencing it for the first time; the idea of being able to act (or react) without willing it can be as hard to absorb as the idea of acting *before* willing it.

In contrast, a voluntary movement originates not with the sensation of heat on a fingertip or a hammer to the knee, but in the brain itself, the seat of consciousness. It has always been assumed that voluntary acts are just what they appear to be: actions resulting from, and therefore following, causative volition. The chain of events is supposed to be as follows:

1. We think about something we desire, possibly on the basis of sensory input.
2. We form the goal of having it and formulate a plan to get it, even if that plan consists of only a simple body movement.
3. We execute the plan.
4. We obtain or fail to obtain the desired object or state.

Step 1 takes place in the cerebral cortex and hypothalamus (the source of drives). Step 2 involves higher-order reasoning and judgment occurring mainly in the frontal lobes. Step 3 involves those parts of the cerebral cortex specialized for voluntary movement, including the primary motor cortex, its associated premotor areas, and other motion-specific neural aggregates. And step 4 feeds back into the limbic system, which registers the satisfaction or frustration of the original drive.

Now let's have a closer look at the distinction between a reflex and a voluntary act. A voluntary act is purposeful and directed towards the completion of a task; a reflex is merely a response to a stimulus. A voluntary act performed in response to a stimulus can vary according to the task being performed; a reflex obviously cannot (because no task is involved). A voluntary act is "endogenous" or internally generated; a reflex is externally stimulated. A voluntary act can be adapted to various circumstances, and its speed and accuracy improved through practice; a reflex is relatively immutable. And because higher levels of the motor system can dissociate the informational content of a stimulus from its capacity to trigger a movement, the information can be voluntarily processed and the movement either permitted or interdicted. With a reflex, there is no such opportunity.

However, the work of Libet *et al.* introduces a new degree of similarity to voluntary and reflex actions: both are to some extent beneath awareness and therefore "subconscious" in that sense of the term, which we shall henceforth replace with "unconscious" to avoid Freudian connotations. In the type of voluntary act studied by Libet and his colleagues, conscious awareness is still technically in control; it precedes the act itself by 0.2 seconds and can in principle "veto" the movement even after the readiness–potential has been initiated. But regarding this point of initiation, one kind of act is no more voluntary than the other. In neither case does the act begin with conscious awareness of the intention to act. The main difference is that while something belatedly purporting to be conscious intent finally appears half a second or more after the beginning of the so–called "voluntary" act, it never appears at all with the reflex. Or if one prefers, the reflex lacks the volitive equivalent of *esprit de l'escalier*.

How are these results to be interpreted? Libet himself feels that since the 200 ms separating conscious intent from muscular contraction is time enough to consciously veto or permit the movement precipitated by the readiness potential, free will remains intact. Thus, although we cannot be held accountable for our apparently unconscious impulses to act, we remain accountable for whether or not we yield to them. However, others have more extreme opinions. For example, C.M. Fisher (2001) speaks for many when he suggests that Libet's research points to a conclusion that "may be reached on the basis of rather elementary observation ... the behavior of humans represents the electrochemical activity of the brain, involuntary, devoid of will and wish. We are automatons."

While Fisher admits that this bleak impression may somehow turn out to be incorrect, he holds it sufficiently likely to be worth serious exploration.

But as regards the question of free will, neither of these interpretations is entirely satisfactory. For while neither Libet nor Fisher holds that the data alone decide the issue, each nevertheless voices a bias regarding the existence of free will, Libet's being affirmative and Fisher's negative. Libet holds free will to be a matter of conscious clearance of prior impulse; Fisher holds free will to be less likely than servitude to deterministic brain chemistry, suggesting that we get used to the idea that we are "automatons". Thus, each one (1) admits that the data are insufficient to decide the free will issue, and (2) unabashedly proceeds to weigh in on the issue anyway, trying to use the data to support his personal opinion on the matter. And in each case, the opinion posits a definite restriction on what most of the human race considers "free will" to be.

In fact, there are other ways to explain the data. For example, the subject may unconsciously choose a target position for the circle and wait for the circle to reach this position before "deciding" to act. In this case, the readiness potential could be merely anticipatory, following the unconscious choice of a target position.

Along much the same lines, the subject may choose a task and formulate an appropriate general plan on a combination of conscious and unconscious levels, delegating certain parts of the execution of this plan, as well as details of scheduling, to the unconscious mind. The unconscious mind would then take responsibility for that which has been delegated to it, executing various subtasks when appropriate and "reminding" the conscious mind of its responsibility to "intend" those acts just before committing them. The conscious mind would automatically take these cues, thereby reserving the right of final authorization and selectively permitting or interdicting the associated unconscious impulses.

The latter explanation incorporates several key concepts. One such concept is the mind's supposed ability to delegate various responsibilities to conscious or unconscious levels of processing, implying that the unconscious mind can to some extent function autonomously, without benefit of direct, step-by-step conscious oversight. Another is the distinction between tasks and subtasks in goal-related processing and behavior. This distinction permits the distinction of an overall task-related decision, e.g. deciding to perform a *sequence* of voluntary hand movements, from constituent subtask-related decisions, e.g. deciding to perform *one* of the hand movements in question.

Yet another such concept is higher-order intentionality, or "intent to intend". For example, intending to perform a sequence of voluntary hand movements amounts to *intending to intend* to perform each of the hand movements in the sequence, and where the latter (lower-order) intentions are generated by the unconscious level of processing, they can in turn be regarded as a *unconscious intentions to consciously intend* to permit or veto the impulses associated with the unconscious intentions themselves. We thus have a kind of "volitional loop" involving two levels of processing, and two levels of intentionality, instead of the single level usually acknowledged ... a multilevel control loop in which the "higher" (conscious) level of volitional processing is insulated from the noise and complexity generated by the "lower", unconscious nuts-and-bolts level, which thus functions to some extent autonomously.

Does this new explanation of volition as a multilevel control loop have any weaknesses? One possible weakness is the fact that because we associate control with consciousness, the very idea of "unconscious volition" seems semantically inconsistent. Relegating any part of a volitional control function to a non-conscious level of mental processing seems to contradict the premise that we possess the freedom to control our actions.

However, a little reflection should reveal that the horse of cognition is already long gone from the barn of consciousness

17

anyway. If the conscious mind, which has an innate need to function within a well-defined conceptual system in order to ensure its informational integrity, were ever made responsible for the details of the complex, tentative, rapid-fire neural dialogue that microscopically relates one well-defined state of consciousness to its successor, cognition would immediately break down like a tired old jalopy. With a catastrophic "kapow!" from its exhaust pipe and a sad sigh of defeat from beneath its hood, it would forcibly retreat into the wakeless sleep of unrealizability. One might as well demand that the output of a computer never be acknowledged until the user has accounted for each of the millions of logical operations by means of which it was generated. Such a demand cannot be met within the bounds of practicality.

The moral of this story should now be obvious. Above, we cited an assumed chain of events comprising a voluntary act. We can now refine that chain as follows:

1. We think about something we desire, possibly on the basis of sensory input. This step amounts to consciously setting general parameters for a supertask or task sequence.

2. We form the goal of possessing the object of desire and formulate a plan to get it. This step amounts to consciously defining the supertask using the parameters of step 1, and automatically delegating as much of it as possible to the unconscious mind.

3. We execute the plan. This step, which may consist of numerous individual tasks or substeps, is executed on a tentative basis by the unconscious mind, which generates impulses that are subjected to conscious oversight as they become sufficiently well-defined to emerge into consciousness.

4. We obtain, or fail to obtain, the desired object or state, at which point the limbic system registers satisfaction or frustration.

Notice that at no point does anything come into being without the involvement of the conscious mind. The conscious mind chooses the overall task and clears or vetoes each subtask as it emerges from the unconscious background to which it was delegated under conscious oversight. In interpreting the Libet experiment, we need simply remember that when the subject consciously accepts the task of generating a sequence of voluntary actions (subtasks) over a given period of time, the entire future contribution of the unconscious mind is automatically requisitioned. At all times, the subject is doing just what he or she has consciously agreed and decided to do, nothing more and nothing less, but with the indispensable help of unconscious faculties without which the conscious mind could not function.

So the real value of the Libet experiment is not that it answers the philosophical question of whether or not free will exists, but merely that it provides data that clarify the operation of free will on the assumption that it *does* exist by elucidating the cerebral dynamics of volition.

What if the brains of experimental subjects, including electrical potentials and conscious ideations, could be monitored without their knowledge by means of a remote scanning procedure, and the experiment were concealed to make them unaware of it? Then they would not be known by the experimenters to have agreed to a specific experimental task, and some of their actions might appear truly spontaneous. It would be interesting to see whether the Bereitschaftspotential still precedes conscious intent in all cases. But if so, could spontaneity be ascertained? It is hard to see how a voluntary act of any kind could be certified as "spontaneous" where responsibility for subtasks is *automatically* delegated to the unconscious mind. Any such act could be related to any purpose consciously adopted at any time in the past, and even the subject may be unable to identify the purpose in question. In principle, the unconscious mind could be involved in a complex, protracted, consciously-authorized sequence of sensorimotor transactions in which the role of a given "spontaneous" act may be quite inscrutable.

What would it take to decide the question of the existence of free will? Because the answer depends on whether the universe evolves in a deterministic or nondeterministic way, this is a metaphysical rather than a merely psychological question. Indeed, answering this question requires an understanding of not only psychology and reality at large, but their logical interface ... the relationship of mind and reality. In other words, it requires a comprehensive theory of reality uniting the subjective and objective sides of existence. Within the overarching framework of such a theory, psychological and neurological phenomena could finally be interpreted in a way that clarifies their deeper philosophical significance.

A Free Will Cyber-Synthesis

That's right, folks ... we're back to free will again. In my defense, I'll say only that if you already believe in free will, then you should want to know as much as possible about how it works, and if you don't, then you have no choice but to resign yourself to your fate and read up on it anyway.

At the start of this book, we discussed Newcomb's Paradox, a controversial prediction paradox that highlights an apparent conflict between two basic principles: the macroscopically apparent linearity of time, whereby time always flows from past to future, and the principle of induction, whereby we form conclusions about reality on the basis of what we observe. We concluded that the relationship between these principles depends on the model of reality in which we interpret them. This was really no surprise, since only certain models of reality support the possibility of the Newcomb scenario in the first place. The surprise, if one exists, is that science has thus far failed to decide which model is correct, and has thus failed to preclude the real existence of a Nukem-like predictor.

Then, in the last chapter, we analyzed a controversial scientific experiment which appears to show that the supposedly voluntary acts of human beings precede any conscious intent to perform them. Although Benjamin Libet, the lead scientist in that experiment, opined that the free will hypothesis survives this finding intact, others believe that it proves mankind a race of automated puppets driven by laws and circumstances beyond our control. We leaned decidedly in favor of Libet in that debate, but again concluded that a final resolution of the issue would require a conceptual framework illuminating the interface between objective reality and the subjective source of volition, namely the mind.

As we saw, it is possible to explain the Libet experiment by positing discrete levels of intentionality, with broader and less immediate levels being relegated to the unconscious mind. Where this generalized unconscious level of self-determination is responsible for the integration of specific acts, it must initiate the preliminary stages of any voluntary act and leave only final clearance to the conscious mind; logically, this is the only way that meaningful volition can work. Indeed, the role of the unconscious is simply to remind the conscious mind of its chosen goals and notify it of an impending opportunity to act in such a way that some long-term goal will be wholly or partially achieved. Unfortunately, it is not easy to see how this applies to Newcomb's paradox.

The Newcomb scenario, in which a predictor (Nukem) unerringly forecasts the behavior of human subjects, and the Libet experiment, in which the subject's own nervous system seems to play the role of "predictor" in beating consciousness to the punch, have more than a little in common: where it is assumed that a future decision process is being passively read rather than actively caused by the predictive agency, they both require that the predictor make a counterintuitive leap through time. In Newcomb's paradox, the predictor must leap into the future and back again with information about a future state or event, while in Libet *et al*, the subject's unconscious mind must leap forward in time in order to "predict" an instance of conscious volition and its outcome (otherwise, it would have to usurp conscious volition entirely).

While the Libet experiment was explained in terms of orders of intentionality arranged in a neural control hierarchy, with higher-order (inclusive) neural relationships controlling lower-order (included) neural relationships, Newcomb's paradox seems to resist such an explanation. This is partially because it is not confined to the brain of a single subject, but deals with the interaction of two non-cooperating subjects in a general environment containing both of them ... an environment not so easily stratified. A major difference between the two scenarios is that in order to win the Newcomb game, Nukem must predict a specific act in advance, while ordinary volition requires merely that reality at large provide alternative outcomes for all possible acts and their timing ... provide "multiple alternative futures" in one of which a given act will automatically result. But to some extent, certain essential features apply to both scenarios. For volition to work in either case, the body and environment must predictably mirror the neural dynamics of the brain. In other words, the picture of reality in our heads must accurately depict reality as it really is, and reality must in turn allow us to form reliable pictures of it.

What "pictures of reality" are we required to have in our heads? First, we must have a picture that represents our bodies. At coarse resolution, this "picture" is a brain map called the *motor homunculus*. If the human body were a puppet and motor nerves its strings, the motor homunculus would be the internal wiring diagram that tells the brain which strings to "pull" to cause particular voluntary movements involving particular parts of the body. Second, we must have an immediate, real-time picture of the environment with which our bodies interact and in which our movements have meaning. Conveniently enough, we ordinarily get such a picture through our eyes and other sense organs. And third, we must have at least a rudimentary understanding of how the world works so that we can predict the outcomes of our actions. This picture is gradually learned by experience and augmented by theoretical reasoning.

Our success in negotiating the often-treacherous road of life depends largely on the accuracy of our pictures of reality and how closely our actions conform to them. To this extent, reality is like the Newcomb predictor. If it "predicts" that our mental pictures of it are faithful and that we will act in conformance with them, it rewards our volition, while if it predicts that our pictures are inadequate, it frustrates us instead. Newcomb's paradox involves an appreciable time interval between prediction and outcome, in the middle of which resides the act that must be predicted. But in the Libet scenario, and in fact for volition in general, the "prediction" is actually *exhaustive provision* for a full range of outcomes. No matter what we do, the world must have our reward or frustration waiting for us in advance; it can make it up on the spot no more than we can choose our goal-oriented actions without advance planning. The burning question is how the world makes this "exhaustive prediction" with such unerring accuracy.

One might object that since it is possible to build a machine that rewards those who use it correctly and frustrates those who do not, and since the universe may be exactly this kind of machine, there is no need for prediction or exhaustive provision. After all, machines function automatically. But this simply begs the question, for the "automatic" operation of any machine depends on preexisting laws of mechanics. Were the laws of mechanics to suddenly break down, so would the machine. So as a first step, the laws of mechanics must be reified and maintained. Unfortunately, reifying and maintaining complete laws of mechanics is a cosmological issue very different from building a machine. When one builds a machine, there is a preexisting nomological framework of which one may take advantage; in building the nomological framework itself, there is not (if there were, then instead of being excused from delivering an explanation, we would simply have to explain the more basic nomological framework).

So the world's exhaustive real-time "prediction" of our actions, and the way it rewards or frustrates us in response, is ultimately synonymous with the laws by which it enforces its own self-consistency. Prediction and control are passive and active sides of the same coin; the laws that allow the world to write itself, i.e. evolve, also allow it to read itself. Thus, the laws of physics double as the means by which the world detects, analyzes and evaluates our actions, and the means by which it "predicts" and readies the outcome. In providing general causal mechanisms by which the world can yield an appropriate result for every action, these laws also provide means by which the world can detect and distinguish one action from another. Without such means, the concept of "action" would have no meaning, and the results of particular actions would not even be regular, much less "appropriate".

In other words, maintaining a set of unbreakable laws, e.g. the laws of physics, amounts to predicting (or exhaustively "meta-predicting") that anyone who tries to break those laws will definitely end up a loser, while predicting different outcomes for different actions entails a set of laws that allow actions and outcomes to be distinguished. Our real-world faith in these laws is analogous to our faith in Nukem's predictive infallibility, and our willing obedience to them is analogous to our acceptance of his predictive powers as a strategic criterion. Perhaps the main difference is that while there may be doubt about whether we can beat Nukem at his own game – his existence may, after all, be incompatible with necessary features of reality – there is very little hope that we can beat reality itself. For while we are physically separate from Nukem the Magnificent, reality contains all living beings and does not permit them to violate its laws.

As we observed, Newcomb's paradox pits the principle of induction against the idea that time flows exclusively from past to future. Either we can reason from local reality to global reality, *or* we can continue to think of time as nothing but an orderly past-to-future sequence, but not both (as we can see from the way these principles support conflicting decisions in the Newcomb scenario). Because the principle of induction permits us to attribute generality to laws active in our local vicinity, it has a "meta-predictive" aspect; it lets us "predict" that observations distant in space or time, regardless of specific content, will be similar to local observations (although this principle is troubled by the aptly-named "problem of induction", we use it out of necessity anyway). But as we have just observed, prediction and control are passive and active sides of the same coin; in some respects, enforcing laws is equivalent to "proactively predicting" the outcomes of a set of possible actions. Thus, the predictive principle of induction is in some respects equivalent to a control function that distributes general laws over space and time.

Do science and mathematics offer us any insight on matters of control? As it happens, all of this is right up the alley of a relatively young field of mathematics called *cybernetics*. Cybernetics, billed by its creator MIT wunderkind Norbert Wiener as "the science of control and communication in animal and machine", pits *freedom* against *constraint* in biological and engineered systems consisting of multiple control strata, with higher strata dominating lower ones in overall self-regulatory relationships. The central dynamical concept is the *feedback loop*, whereby actions or instructions issued by a control object affect a controlled object, which sends information on its new state back to the controller, which then updates its routine to further maintain or adjust the state of the controllee (and round and round they go in more or less complex flow diagrams). Cybernetics, the mathematical bedrock of the computer age, is about as close as mainstream science has yet come to forming a mechanical picture of purposive, goal-oriented behavior.

However, cybernetics goes only so far in its explanations, confining itself to mechanical or biological systems more or less analogous to electronic computers. Regarding the pre-mechanical or metaphysical phase of control and communication, the phase concerned with selecting, enacting and distributing laws and forces that allow machines to be built, cybernetics yields only silence. Where a system is completely self-contained, cybernetics explains it intrinsically on a mechanical level through internal feedback; where a system is not self-contained, cybernetics pursues mechanical control and feedback past the systemic boundary into the environment. But beyond this, cybernetics makes the usual round of too-convenient assumptions, e.g. that it is possible to regress from one control level to another *ad infinitum*, and that because explanatory regression through successive control strata never terminates, pre-mechanical or metaphysical considerations need never be addressed. The system of interest is simply placed within a nested series of mechanical systems-within-systems through which control and feedback can be plotted.

But the universe is more than a mechanical system; as we have established, it is a nomological "predictor" of all that it contains. The universe is so powerful a predictor that unlike Nukem or one of his subjects, it does not even need to know what specific act a person will commit in advance; it can simply allow for all possible acts by providing a possible outcome for every one of them. As Newcomb's paradox reminds us, we usually think of time as one-dimensional and one-directional, a linear dimension along which the present moves from past to future. Unfortunately, this kind of time is simply too limited to support nomological meta-prediction, providing means and explanation for neither its own existence not that of volition. Such an explanation, along with that which is to be explained, requires the existence of a control level above that of time itself . . . a level representing hidden temporal structure.

What is the nature of this stratification? Cybernetics can offer some pointers. First, let's try to get a cybernetic view of a generic competitive scenario. Consider a 1 or 2-player game based on a computer simulation or *virtual reality*. There are two control levels in this game, one simulated and one simulative, to which correspond the roles of "subject" and "programmer". The programmer, being in charge of a computer on whose monitor runs a simulation containing the subject, controls the subject and his fate. In fact, as far as the subject is concerned, the programmer is a veritable "master of time", having the ability to fast-forward, reverse and replay the simulation at will. Therefore, the object of the game is to occupy the role of programmer. In addition, there is a third "role" to consider: that of the game's Designer. Because the Designer makes the rules that the player(s) must obey, this is an important role indeed.

There are four possible positions in the 2-player version of this game:

1. Player A and player B are both in the role of subject. In this case, neither controls the game, and it's a toss-up.
2. A is in the role of programmer and B is in the role of subject. In this case, A controls the game and therefore wins.
3. B is in the role of programmer and A is in the role of subject. In this case, B controls the game and therefore wins.
4. A and B are both in the role of programmer. In this case, both A and B control the game, and because neither controls the other, they are forced to cooperate. This leads to a draw (or a mutual win or loss, depending on how the game is structured).

Now let's see who or what we can cast in these roles. First, consider Newcomb's paradox. Where Nukem is player A and his subject is player B, the Newcomb scenario corresponds to position 2 above. Nukem – who always wins – is definitely in the role of programmer, and because he determines the outcome whether or not the subject chooses to cooperate, he is always in a higher control stratum (this precludes position 4). What is it about Nukem that makes it possible for him to win this game 100% of the time? That, of course, is a question for science fiction authors. For present purposes, the important part is what cybernetics tells us about where he must be sitting: somewhere above the subject in a control hierarchy.

Now let's consider the Libet experiment. In this scenario, there is only one player, the experimental subject. In the *solitaire* version of this game, a lone player must play both roles, and the only possible object of the game is therefore self-control. But what is self-control? It is precisely that which enables voluntary action. That is, the experimental subject, in attempting to commit a string of voluntary acts, is trying to simultaneously put himself in the roles of programmer and subject so that he can control and perform his own movements.

According to our explanation for the peculiar timing of the neural events involved in this endeavor, the subject executes his duties as "programmer" in two phases relegated to his unconscious and conscious mind respectively.

Notice what this says about the relationship between the Newcomb and Libet scenarios. In displacing the player from the role of programmer, Nukem is either usurping the player's self-control and thus depriving him of free will, or making sure that whatever self-control the player insists on retaining turns out to be disappointingly unprofitable. In the latter case, Nukem must do something more impressive than merely controlling the player; he must control the contents of a certain box to ensure that the player is robbed of success and thereby punished for his or her willfulness. In other words, in making his prediction, Nukem must control some part of the subject-environment complex in a way that violates our intuitive notions of time and causality.

What about the Designer of the game? Because the Designer makes the rules, and because rules are analogous to laws, the Designer's real-world analogue is the universal principle responsible for selecting, distributing and enforcing the laws of reality, and thereby setting the stage for volition. This represents a higher level of control than those occupied by programmer and subject; the programmer derives his "programmatic" ability to see into and/or control future states of reality, subjective and objective alike, wholly from the Designer. That this applies to volition in general should now be clear as a bell.

(Of course, there still remains a problem: we have not yet decided whether or not free will really exists. But if the set-up were all that easy, the free will question would have been definitively answered a long time before we ever got around to it.)

Where does it all lead? To exciting new extensions of cybernetics and other fields of mathematics? To new inroads in physics and cosmology? To new insights regarding theological concepts like God, the human soul, and ethical refinements based on an enhanced understanding of good and evil?

As a matter of fact, yes it does. But why not leave a little something for later?

Solutions for the Problems of Free Will, Good and Evil, Consciousness and God

For three chapters now, I've subjected you to merciless philosophical, neurobiological and mathematically-oriented disquisitions on free will, even arranging your involuntary participation in a virtual game show and a scientific experiment. As a reward for your long suffering, we'll now try to extract some momentous implications from the little thread we've got going. Specifically, we're going to show that free will definitely exists. Then we're going to explain that while this doesn't necessarily mean that human beings possess it in any immediate sense, there are good reasons to believe that they do. And then we're going to discuss a few important philosophical corollaries.

First, let's review the virtual reality game described in the last chapter. The point of introducing this 1- or 2-player Game was to provide a standard analytical framework for Newcomb's paradox and the Libet delayed-choice experiment. The Game has two control levels respectively inhabited by a "subject" and "programmer". The subject inhabits a simulated world under the control of the programmer, who is able to fast-forward, reverse and replay the simulation at will. The first step toward winning the Game is to occupy the role of programmer and thereby gain control of the outcome (sadly, there are not yet any detailed instructions for doing this). The *solitaire* version requires that a lone player play both roles, making self-control, i.e. personal volition, the only possible object of the Game.

In addition, we defined a third "role", that of the Game Designer who makes the rules that the player(s) must obey. These rules include the laws of causality that operate on each level, and the laws governing the relationships among control levels. Because the Designer in effect occupies a third control level, there are three control levels altogether. Control flows downward through these levels, from Designer to programmer to subject. Due to the quality and quantity of control associated with the role of Designer, the Designer has a clear theological analogue: God. In the context of the Game, denying the existence of the Designer would amount to asserting that despite the complex structural organization of the Game, it is random in origin.

Let's begin by reviewing a few historical viewpoints regarding the free will issue. First, we have the idea, dear to the hearts of most of us and especially to those who framed the U.S. Constitution and other rational codes of law and ethics, that human beings have free will. While we acknowledge that there are laws of causality that apply to everyone regardless of time or place – e.g. "for every action there is an equal and opposite reaction" – these are not sufficient to control our behavior, leaving us free to "make our own laws" when it comes to our personal preferences. This corresponds to the *solitaire* version of the Game, but with a tacit restriction on the fast-forward, reverse and replay options: they are usually considered to be exclusively "mental", i.e. confined to our respective thought processes.

Then we have *determinism*, the idea that the laws of causality determine our every move. Determinism holds that we resemble billiard balls rolling around and colliding on a barroom pool table, bouncing off each other under the impulses imparted to us by environmental cue sticks. Like the cue sticks themselves, the internal impulses triggered in our minds and bodies by external stimuli are completely motivated by the laws of physics, reductively including the laws of genetics, biology and psychology. There is no causal gap in which free will can find a toehold. This corresponds to a version of the Game in which the Designer leaves no open controls for the programmer to use; the structure of the Game, as fixed by the Designer, absolutely controls the simulation and the subject.

(While Laplace, widely considered the father of determinism, once remarked to Napoleon that a deterministic universe "has no need" of a Designer, he thereby left himself with no way to account for the mathematical laws of causality offered as a replacement.)

Juxtaposed to determinism is indeterminism or *randomism*, the idea that causality is only an illusion and that everything, including human behavior, is utterly random. This represents a bizarre mutation of the Game in which one or both of the following conditions hold:

1. The Designer is absent, dead, or out to lunch; the Game, and its rules of causality and interlevel control, exist solely by "chance". An obvious drawback of this viewpoint is that it fails to account for the probabilistic laws of chance themselves.

2. The rules of causality do not exist at all; they are merely *supposed* to exist by the subject and break down where the subject's powers of self-delusion end, beyond which point chance rules openly. In other words, when a subject fancies that he is "making a decision", he is really rolling the dice, and somehow, his sequential delusions of intent, action and outcome perfectly match the dice roll. This, of course, seems to give a whole new meaning to the term "improbable".

In addition to free will, determinism and randomism, there is another doctrine worth considering: *predestination*. Predestination is the idea that God can look at a person, measure his or her tendencies towards goodness and/or badness, predict how the person will decide to behave in his or her particular setting, and consign that person's soul to heaven or hell on that basis. Where God's insight relies on the existence of laws that transform information on a person's innate tendencies and environmental conditions to information on behavior – these laws are ostensibly what He uses make

His prediction – predestination amounts to determinism with a theological twist. Where God determines both the personality of the subject and the laws that determine his behavior, this boils down to the following scenario: God makes a person, sizes up His handiwork, says either (a) "Man, am I good!" or (b) "Screwed up again!", and tosses His newest creation onto the pile marked "Heaven Bound" or "Born To Lose". If you happen to be a Calvinist, this is your lot – or should that be lotto? – in life.

However, there is another strain of predestination, favored by (e.g.) the Roman Catholic Church, that does not rely on determinism. According to this version of the doctrine, God might instead do one of the following:

1. Scan the subject for freely-formed higher-order intent. As we recall, persistent higher-order intent is what the experimental subject generates in agreeing to participate in the Libet experiment and move his hand repeatedly at will. To capture the theological flavor of predestination, compare this to "what the subject generates in freely selling his soul to the devil and agreeing to commit a lifelong string of felonies and misdemeanors".

2. Let the subject play out and determine his own simulation, then use the rewind control to back up to the subject's moment of birth and invisibly stamp him "Accepted" or "Rejected". In this case, God is simply jumping forward in time to observe the subject's timeline, and then jumping back through time to affix the proper invisible label to its origin. This kind of predestination leaves room for free will.

Notice that where free will is absent, the mind is reduced to a mere byproduct of deterministic material reality. Consciousness, including the psychological sensation of intentionality and self-awareness in general, becomes a kind of meaningless sideshow compulsively played by our irrelevant "minds", as we are forced to call them, to interpret that which they cannot affect. The idea that the mind is just a side effect of objective physical processes is called *epiphenomenalism*. One can, of course, split hairs over the question of whether the mind is truly intrinsic to our material brains and bodies, or just extra metaphysical baggage that is somehow tied to them by some kind of ethereal thread. But either way, if intentionality has nothing to do with the structure of reality, then matter and the laws of physics are all that really count. Our "minds" are just along for the ride.

We've enumerated the above scenarios to show that the cybernetic paradigm, involving feedback among layers of control, clarifies the distinctions among traditional approaches to volition. This is a bit surprising; while cybernetics is a respected branch of modern science, the position of the scientific establishment as a whole is evidently nowhere near as sophisticated. It is based on a naive understanding of causality which holds that with respect to anything not locked into a determinative causal relationship, randomness prevails. For example, modern physics characterizes reality on three scales: the overall cosmic scale, the macroscopic scale of ordinary objects, and the ultramicroscopic scale of atoms and subatomic particles, to which it applies the rules of relativity, classical mechanics and quantum mechanics respectively (where relativity is understood as a classical theory). Unfortunately, the dichotomy between "classical" and "quantum" reality is essentially the same as that between causality and randomness or determinacy and indeterminacy. It thus effectively excludes all of the above scenarios except determinism and randomism, leaving the existence of free will with no apparent possibility of scientific explanation.

Determinacy and indeterminacy ... at first glance, there seems to be no middle ground. Events are either causally connected or they are not, and if they are not, then the future would seem to be utterly independent of the past. Either we use causality to connect the dots and draw a coherent picture of time, or we settle for a random scattering of independent dots without spatial or temporal pattern and thus without meaning. But there is another possibility after all: *self-determinacy*. One can be the author of one's own personal "causality", setting up a volitional feedback loop between one's will and one's goals, where "goals" include everything from spontaneous bodily movements to the fruits of long labor and well-laid, well-executed plans.

Self-determinism is a rather subtle concept. It means that one determines one's own path *independently* of general laws of causality, where "independence" describes a situation in which one is constrained by, but also free to exploit at will, the laws of physics and biology. It therefore implies that neither randomness nor the laws of causality have the final word in the determination of reality; there is enough room between them for human beings, who are themselves parts of reality, to "get a word in edgewise". But how is this possible, given that the general laws of causality, linear and chaotic, are the only things short of "quantum randomness" that can possibly account for the structure of reality as a whole? It is possible only if there is more to the overall structure of reality than randomness or the laws of causality can fully determine, and only if human beings possess a means of shaping this extra structure at will.

To expand further on the concept of volition, we must take a closer look at its meaning. When we do, we find that "meaning" is precisely what volition entails. Concisely, to "have meaning" is to play a critical role, to make a crucial difference, in something of value, where *value* is reckoned in practical, emotional, intellectual or spiritual (edificative) terms. So to be meaningful, volition must enable one to advance, in a way transcending the laws of causality and imparting value beyond that of causality alone, toward freely-chosen goals which themselves possess meaning or value. But for goals to have meaning, *the system in which they reside* must have meaning. If reality were meaningless, there would be no basis on which to ascribe meaning to anything in it; "valueless value" is no value at all. So if meaningful volition exists, reality itself must have meaning, and there must be an objective, meaningful scale on which its value can be gauged.

But now there arises a problem: in order to be "objective", something must be *real*. On what real, objective scale can reality be measured? If we define "reality" in the most straightforward and tautological way, namely as "that which contains all and only that which is real", no such thing as an external scale is possible. For by our definition, anything real enough to quantify reality from the *outside* is already included in reality and therefore on the *inside*! Since this is a logical contradiction, the idea that reality can be externally evaluated is logically invalid. This implies that in order to possess meaningful existence and thus be capable of supporting meaningful volition, reality must be "self-evaluating". All of its value scales must be internal to it, and its meaning must be intrinsic.

In fact, we can go somewhat farther. In the traditional view of science, that which is not random must be created or selected according to ambient (externally extended) principles of causality. But where external causality requires external scales against which to be defined, it can no more possess real existence than the external scales themselves. Again, anything real enough to affect reality from the outside is already included in reality and therefore on the inside, and since this is a logical contradiction, the idea of external causality is *a priori* invalid with respect to reality. This implies that in order to possess meaningful existence and therefore support meaningful volition, reality must be "self-caused". But this comprehensive kind of self-causation entails an even deeper form of self-determination than that usually associated with volition; reality must not only determine its own structure independently of external causality, but must do so starting with nothing but itself! In other words, the universe must possess a global analogue of free will that lets it internally define and calibrate the very scale on which its intrinsic value is internally measured.

But wait a minute. Aren't we ignoring the possibility that the universe is simply "random", i.e. uncaused? Not really, for externally speaking, that's exactly what it is! In deducing that the universe is unaffected by external causality, we find that it is externally acausal or "random" in that specific sense of the term. The operative distinction, of course, is that which holds between internal and external causality. And since our observations of a coherent, well-regulated, profoundly ordered universe rule out the possibility of internal randomness from the start – there is no way that a system as coherent and complex as the real universe can be accurately described as "randomly disordered" – we've got the issue of cosmic randomness sufficiently well-covered for present purposes.

So reality, being self-determinative but externally uncon-strained, possesses a global, self-enabling analogue of free will that generates its own means of realization. If these means can be utilized by human beings *within* reality, then human beings possess free will, and because they are included in reality, they can use it to contribute to the realization of the global Self-structuring imperative. On the other hand, even if human beings cannot avail themselves of free will, they can still be used *by* it for the same purpose. In either case, human beings are integral parts of reality that contribute to its structure, and must either be using the inherent freedom of reality to do so, or be freely used as tools by some higher level of realty to the same end. So while the using-versus-used question remains up in the air, one fact has nevertheless been rationally established: whether it belongs exclusively to the universe or to man as well, *free will exists*. (Q.E.D.)

Now let's look at some convincing cybernetic evidence that we participate in the self-creation of reality. Because intentional self-creation entails an internal stimulus-response dynamic consisting of feedback, any self-configuring system needs internal sensors (agents, internal self-proxies) capable of not only recognizing and affecting its state from local inter-nal vantages, but of responding to higher-level instructions tending to enforce global structural criteria. Moreover, the system must possess a stratified utility function allowing it and its agents to prefer one possible future over another. Human beings and other intelligent life forms are useful to reality on both of these counts. So the first criterion of reality is the possibility, and in fact the inevitability, of the existence of "sensors" just like us ... sensors with an advanced capacity to recognize, evaluate and respond to internal states of the system.

How, in general, would the universe self-configure? It would select itself from a set of internally-generated, internally-refined structural possibilities in order to maximize its self-defined value. In the (somewhat inadequate) terminology of quantum mechanics, this set of possibilities is called its *quantum wave function* or QWF, and the utility-maximizing self-selection principle is traditionally called *teleology*. In exploiting this self-actualization mechanism, human beings would select their specific goals from the global QWF according to their own specific self-selection principles or "teleses". In the course of being realized, these individual teleses would interfere with teleology (and each other) in a constructive or destructive way, depending on whether they and their specific methods of implementation (modes of interference) are teleologically consistent or inconsistent. In this way, the "good", or teleologically constructive, may be distinguished from the "bad", or teleologically destructive. I.e., free will would give human beings a real choice between good and evil ... a choice like that which we already seem to possess.

For example, say that you choose great personal wealth as your goal. Whether this goal is inherently good, bad or indifferent depends on whether or not its realization would necessarily lead to a net increase or decrease in global utility or value, and thus interfere constructively or destructively with teleology (in which cases it is good or bad respectively). Suppose that it is not inherently bad. Then whether its *specific realization* is bad depends on whether your means of realizing it will be prohibitively costly to the aggregate consisting of you, those near you, mankind as a whole and the entire Planet Earth (if they are, then the ends do not quantitatively justify the means). As we recall from the last two installments, any goal that can only be reached through a more or less complex sequence of actions is assigned to a higher, long-term level of intentionality that suggests and coordinates one's actions in light of it, with the subject retaining "power of veto". To qualify as "good" or at least "indifferent", you must use your power of veto to ensure that your individual actions meet the same teleological consistency criterion that applies to your overall goal.

But hold on there – doesn't the question of good and evil automatically evoke the topic of theology? Of course it does. "God" is just the name we give to the protean creative principle that generates and enforces teleology, or equivalently, that Entity whose "Will" equals teleology. Since this is the same entity whose self-structuring operations are guided by teleology, namely reality, we have a measure of equivalence between reality and God. This makes sense for the following reason: reality can be mathematically modeled as a *Self-Configuring Self-Processing Language* (SCSPL), a dynamic system possessing not just a global analogue of volition, i.e. teleology, but a global analogue of self-awareness as well, i.e. SCSPL self-processing. So where "consciousness" is an attribute with active and passive dimensions amounting to volition and self-awareness, "God" and "reality" are equally good answers for the question "What entity possesses the global form of consciousness described by SCSPL?" In other words, it's just as we might have expected: God is the ultimate reality.

This, of course, brings us back to the notion that "God" is a real-world analogue of the Designer in our cybernetic Game. But now the game is reality, its object is the Designer's own Self-creation, and any number of players occupying any number of lower control strata are just participants in the Self-configuration of the reality they inhabit (for now, we'll ignore the long-running debate over whether God can inject Himself into the bottom-level simulation as a "messiah", simply answering "yes" and leaving it at that). When we use the freedom we inherit from reality at large to properly choose our teleses and exercise our powers of veto, we favorably tilt the balance between teleology and anti-teleology, good and evil, and thus inherit meaning in the bargain. This meaning enriches our lives and sustains the conscious identities with which reality has endowed us as its internal proxies.

Notice that our answer for the question of free will has brought with it the answers for some bonus questions: "What are good and evil?", "What is consciousness?" and "What is God?" (We've left out a few technical details, of course, but that's only because we need to reserve a few surprises for future essays.) Given that you could spend your entire life's salary on popular and academic literature and still not get a tentative logic-driven answer for even one of these questions, how's *that* as a payoff for four straight chapters on the science and philosophy of volition?

By any reasonable measure, you've done quite well for yourself.

PART II

On the Perils of Metaphysical
Skysurfing Without a Parachute

or *"Je n'avais pas besoin de cette hypothèse-là"*

Although we often forget to act like it, human beings are indisputably the brightest bulbs on the evolutionary tree. So in describing where we stand in relation to the rest of the animal kingdom, we tend to stress our intellects, asserting that we are on top of the food chain, the clothes chain and the housing chain because virtually every other species that crawls, hops, swims or flies is a dim bulb by comparison. No matter how much stronger, faster, or keener of eye, ear and nose other species may be – and pound for pound, they are virtually all much stronger, faster or sharper-sensed than we – we are the ones who climbed to the top of the evolutionary ladder ... spectacularly outsmarted the biological competition ... cleaned up in the All-Time Grey Matter Sweepstakes.

So much for the creatures that preceded us on the timeline of creation. What of those which came after us ... the creatures of metal, plastic and silicon that we birthed to aid us in our physical and mental labors? Here, the same applies *a fortiori*. Regardless of horsepower, clock rate or memory capacity, none of our machines can hold a candle to even the weakest among us. For machines merely obey the laws of physics, while we alone can study, formulate and manipulate those laws to our own advantage. Ours are the hands on switch and dial, on mouse and keyboard, on tiller and wheel, on gas hose and power plug. Without our protection and guidance, even our most durable machines would be naturally selected for fast extinction. We are human not just because of our intelligence, but because of our will to control ... our will to supremacy.

So far, so good. But then we collectively make a daring leap. Not satisfied with our quantitative superiority on the scales of intelligence and control, we philosophically transform it into a qualitative difference setting us forever apart from other animate and inanimate entities. Historically, this difference was boldly expressed in statements like "human beings have souls; machines and the lower animals do not." Because this is an age of science, and science pretends to have no use for that which cannot be empirically demonstrated, such statements are now heard a bit less frequently. But the assumed difference lingers on in our minds, implicit but ineffable, a tacit but unbreakable confidence in the unique nature of human consciousness and its sovereign place in the eternal hierarchy of being.

This putative qualitative difference is central to our ethos. It justifies the lion's share of earthly resources that we take, use and waste. It is our philosophical "license to kill" ... to overpopulate the planet, to extinguish other forms of life, to pollute the environment. It is central to what we call the "meaning of life" and to our own meanings as individuals. And because it is absolutely essential to our collective self-importance, we like to think of it as anything but accidental. Indeed, if it has any real significance, it cannot be a quirk of fate, a chance pattern of spots on the cosmic dice. Our claim to preeminence must be based not on mere physical dominion, but on *metaphysical distinctiveness*. We are what and who we are because this is how it was *meant to be*. Despite having disposed of pre-Copernican anthropocentric cosmology several centuries ago, we yet embrace a metaphysical analogue of it that refuses to die.

Unfortunately, certain trends in science threaten to kill it nonetheless. Take, for example, our vaunted intelligence. Dolphins, porpoises and other cetaceans display playfulness, task learning ability and mental agility impressive even to humans. A strain of lab mice called "Doogie mice" – remember

Doogie Hauser? – are bred for high densities of brain proteins called NR2B receptors that enhance their performance on task-based animal intelligence tests, narrowing the IQ gap between humans and rodents. Researchers on human intelligence are even now locating human genes associated with high IQ, thus accumulating the knowledge to genetically engineer super-smart children like the precocious Doogie himself. And pharmaceutical companies are already analyzing the effects of such genes to develop "smart drugs" expected to cause IQ spikes of up to 50 extra points. This gives rise to a disturbing question: how special is intelligence when it can be dispensed from a bottle or syringe to humans and animals alike?

But wait! Even if task performance has a biological basis, could there not be something special in our use of *language*? Well, not necessarily. Human linguistic ability has been localized to specific brain modules, like Broca's and Wernicke's areas, that seem to have counterparts in the brains of some animals. For example, a monkey's premotor cortex contains an area known as F5 that is considered analogous to Broca's area and contains special cells, called "mirror neurons", that appear to be present in human brains as well. Meanwhile, certain African grey parrots can seemingly hold rudimentary but meaningful conversations involving both quality and quantity. And great apes like gorillas and chimpanzees, with whom we share up to 98% of our DNA, regularly communicate using sign language vocabularies of thousands of words ... if certain studies are correct, enough to rival the functional vocabularies of many humans.

But does primate language use not differ from ours in its lack of *empathy*, and is empathy not a distinctively human "spiritual attribute"? Not by the look of certain recent findings. Having noted that the brain of a human observer generates excitatory patterns that mirror patterns in the brain of someone performing a task, a team of researchers has examined monkey brains and found a new class of brain cells in which such mirrored patterns reside. (Can you guess their location? That's right ... F5.) The sympathetic firing of these "mirror neurons" bids fair to be the neural equivalent of empathy. No longer is empathy a moral and spiritual attribute of personhood, a *je ne sais quoi* of human social interaction. Like the jerk of a tapped knee and the dilation of a pupil in sudden darkness, empathy appears to be just another biological phenomenon reducible to the ubiquitous *pas de trois* of proton, neutron and electron in random chunks of matter.

So much for intelligence and empathy as evidence for human spiritual ascendancy. What of spirituality itself? As it happens, world literature affords several telling adumbrations of modern scientific research on this topic. In his tragicomic novel *The Idiot*, Fyodor Dostoievsky described the expansive feeling of beatitude experienced by his protagonist Prince Myshkin just prior to the onset of epileptic seizures. Insofar as Dostoievsky himself suffered from epilepsy, these fictionalized accounts seem to have been taken directly from the author's personal experience ... and the great Russian novelist was far from alone. Many patients afflicted with temporal lobe epilepsy have reported that when a spell overtakes them, they "see God" or experience "enlightenment". Searching for the explanation, neurologists were finally able to find a connection between temporal lobe epilepsy and spontaneous religious feelings: epileptic seizures can stimulate a structure called the "God module" (!) in the temporal–limbic region of the human brain.

Inspired by such successes, science is now looking at the neurological correlates of religious experience in general. This emerging field already has a name, *neuro-theology*, and a central premise: that feelings of spirituality are due to the genetic wiring of the human nervous system. To illustrate, neuro-theological researchers recently conducted an unusual experiment in which a Tibetan Buddhist tugged on a strand of twine as he entered a state of meditative transcendence. Upon this prearranged signal, a researcher injected a radioactive tracer into an IV line attached to the subject's arm and scanned his brain with a sophisticated machine known as

SPECT. SPECT's circuits registered a dramatic reduction in neural activity within a specialized region at the top rear of his brain ... an area known to be responsible for translating sensory data into comprehension of the boundary between self and environment. Having shut down his "self-delimiter module" by meditative sensory deprivation, the subject had destroyed the subjective distinction between internal and external reality and become "one with the universe".

The effect is nonsectarian. According to brain scans, praying makes Franciscan nuns feel "oneness with God" by suppressing the activity of their self-delimiter modules. And the neural aspects of religion are by no means confined to meditation and prayer. A 1997 Japanese study showed that the rhythmic repetition of ritual chanting and dancing causes a certain brain component, the hypothalamus, to generate feelings of serenity or arousal. For example, while repeatedly chanting a mantra transports a yogi to a state of deep inner calm, Sufi mystics feverishly dance themselves to states of excitement in which they feel like "live wires" crackling with the infinite energy of the universe. But does this provide evidence for anything of an objectively transcendental nature? The response of neurotheology to this question is just that of Laplace to Napoleon regarding the existence of God: *"Je n'avais pas besoin de cette hypothèse-là."* Given the physical nature of that which is to be explained, there is no need for such a hypothesis.

The elevated status of human consciousness grows ever more precarious upon the swaying tightrope of metaphysical distinctiveness. First came evidence for the physical basis of consciousness in the various aphasias and apraxias associated with brain lesions; then came the frontal assault of operant conditioning on free will; now we have brain-scanned nuns and the possibility of genetically engineered intellectual and spiritual "geniuses". Intelligence, language, empathy, spirituality ... all of our claims to metaphysical distinctiveness seem to be falling beneath the heartless scythe of physical reductionism. So where will we go now, at the dawn of the New

Millennium, for renewed confirmation of our "specialness" in the scheme of things?

Fortunately, we are not yet facing an ideological dead end. For it seems that just ahead on the intellectual horizon looms a new science of metaphysics ... a logical framework in which the importance of humankind is unthreatened by reductionism, and in which the significance of human feelings and emotions is uncompromised by their correlation with lowly biological processes. Rather than declaring us the abject slaves of natural laws beyond our control, this framework yields a new understanding of space and time in which the very laws of physics can be viewed as an expression of our minds. Granted, this framework remains hidden despite its portentious approach. But if its ongoing delay contributes to our collective store of humility, perhaps this is not entirely a bad thing.

For now, we may simply observe that science consists of building accurate conceptual models of the world, and that the theory of models has thus become a crucial ingredient of scientific reality. Perhaps the most distinctive characteristic of model theory is its use of "metalanguages", or languages that talk about languages, to analyze the mappings, or correspondences, between scientific theories and their universes of discourse. Logically, such metalanguages amount to relationships between theoretical cognition and perceptual reality ... or with a slight frame shift, between the mind and the real world of scientific observations. Because these relationships do more than just describe reality – because they turn out to be primary conditions of its existence – they distribute over it on all scales, uniting the ubiquitous subjective and objective sides of its nature. The universal distribution of these relationships implies the existence of a homogeneous cognitive and perceptual medium embracing the real universe and propagating the influence of our minds throughout the cosmos.

Examined within the distinctive logical structure of this medium, time and causality turn out not to be confined to the familiar past-to-future direction. Instead, the future-to-past direction becomes important as well. The bidirectionality of time implies that the universe is in a state of extended spatiotemporal self-superposition, each of its serial configurations, as defined at each successive moment of time, in contact with all others. At first glance, this seems to imply that the universe is completely determined ... that as Laplace believed, *every* state of the universe is implicit in *any* state. But not only is such an assumption unnecessary, it would ultimately lead to intractable inconsistencies. In fact, the logical structure of spacetime provides the universe with the wherewithal of being, endowing it with self-creative freedom and permitting it to rise from a sea of undifferentiated ontological potential.

What does this have to do with neuro-theology? Insofar as God is generally defined as the Prime Mover or first principle of reality, God is by definition real, and thus a part of the real universe. And because this first principle is by definition primary – because there is by definition no preexisting reality to contain it – reality cannot properly include it. So the real universe must coincide with God; scientific knowledge is theological knowledge, and science a form of theology. It follows that our ability to use science to better the plight of our species – our capacity to know God and to help others know God – is part of what makes us "special". And where true science is a key ingredient of our claim to metaphysical distinctiveness, our place in the hierarchy of being cannot be threatened by science done thoroughly, correctly, and without *a priori* restrictions on our rôle in the scheme of things.

But what is that rôle? Where does humanity fit into the scheme even now being revealed to us by science ... we, who have lately found ourselves reduced to the wearing of metaphysical sackcloth? It turns out that in a certain precise sense, we are microcosms, images of the universe within the universe. And because of the symmetric connection between source and image, cosmos and microcosm, we function as agents through whom the universe realizes its being. We are its children and heirs, poised on the threshold of adulthood and charged with shaping Destiny itself, with helping the living universe choose its form and content from a background of undifferentiated potential. Though eons removed from the moment of creation, we actively retrodict it, sending the power of our minds back through time to help the Prime Mover, our parent and provider, self-creatively embody the universe we inhabit.

Let us do well our filial duty. For by the partial identity of parent and child, we serve ourselves and each other in the bargain.

A *Very* Brief History of Time

I just had a chance encounter with a garden slug, and it got me thinking about time.

In this ostensibly inanimate, impersonal universe, a garden is a miracle. All the more so is a *garden* slug, an animal that can extract sufficient energy from the garden's vegetable matter to move from place to place under its own power. When one is in the right mood, watching the shimmering spotted slug slide over the mulch evokes the miracle of biology in all its splendor; the creature's pulsating aliveness is hypnotic. But then one recovers his bearings and realizes that this is only, after all, a garden slug, and that the ladder of biology goes much higher. The miracle of life has culminated in one's own species, *man*. Unlike the slug, whose nervous system has barely enough complexity to let it interface with the environment, a man's nervous system, nucleated by the adaptive and inventive human brain, can abstractly model its surroundings and project itself consciously and creatively through *time*.

A slug can learn. The small neural network that serves as its brain can be modified by sensory input from its environment, and the slug's behavior modified accordingly. To this extent, the slug "remembers" the input. But because its simple brain cannot form an internal model of its changing relationship with the garden, the slug cannot recognize its memories as "changes"; the state of its nervous system at any given moment can pass for all that it has ever known. Because the neural function by which the slug identifies *self* is instinctual and perceptual as opposed to cognitive – because the slug "defines itself" strictly by nonreflective instinctual processing of environmental stimuli – the dependent neural function *time* is limited to here-and-now. The slug recognizes no past self or future self on which to define an extended temporal relationship.

As the slug's primitive example shows, our awareness of time depends on the extent to which our mental models of reality reflect *change*. To see an object change, one must recall its former state for comparison to its present state, and to do that, one must recall one's former perception of it. Because perception is an interaction between self and environment, this amounts to bringing one's *former self* into conjunction with one's *present self*. That past and present selves can be brought into conjunction across a temporal interval implies that momentary selves remain sufficiently alike to be conjoined; that they can intersect at any given moment to compare content means that the intersection is changeless. So when self is generalized as *the intersection of all momentary selves*, it acquires a property called *time invariance*. It is the rock of perception, the unchanging observation post from which the net of temporal connections is cast and to which it remains anchored. Indeed, it is the fabric from which the net is woven, its relationship with the environment serving as the 86universal template for all temporal relationships.

Through learning, mental models *of* time evolve *in* time. As the brain's neural connections are modified and the strengths of existing connections are adjusted to account for new information regarding both self and environment – as it *learns* – its model of time changes as a *function* of time. In other words, the model changes with that which is modeled. If the brain is smart enough, then it can model itself in the process of being changed, and depict its own learning process as a higher level of time. But even as the self absorbs its educational history and deepens its reflexive understanding, it remains static at its core. Otherwise, it would lose temporal cohesion and fall apart. Since self is static, time too should possess a static description that does not change in the temporal flow it describes (if time were the water flowing in a river, then a static description of time would be analogous to the rocky banks that determine the river's course).

Such a description arises by *abstraction*. As cognitive models become more sophisticated, cognition becomes increasingly abstract; concepts become increasingly independent of the particular objects they describe. Among the first things to be abstracted are space and time. The most general abstract system incorporating both is a *language*. Although the term "language" usually refers to a natural language like English, it is actually more general. Mathematically, a *formal language* consists of three ingredients: a set of elements to be combined as strings (e.g., symbols, memes), a set of structural rules governing their arrangement in space, and a set of grammatical rules governing their transformations in time. Together, the latter two ingredients form the *syntax* of the language. It follows that neural, cognitive-perceptual, and physical systems can be described as languages, and the laws which govern them as their syntaxes. On a subjective level, time itself can be abstractly characterized as the *grammar* of the joint language of cognition and perception. The rules of this grammar are the general ingredients of subjective time.

Because time is defined in terms of transformations among spatial arrangements of objects, it is conceptually entwined with space. Thus, it is actually part of a linguistic complex called *spacetime*. Spatiotemporal relations exist on many levels; if level one consists of simple relationships of objects in space and time, then level two consists of relationships of such relationships, and so on. Because logic is *stratified* in much the same way, one can say that time is stratified in a manner corresponding to predicate logic. This must be true in any case, since any meaningful description of time is logically formulated. Spatiotemporal stratification allows time to be viewed on various scales corresponding to ascending series of contexts: e.g., personal awareness, interpersonal relationships, social evolution, evolutionary biology, and so on. The histories of people, institutions, cultures, and species are nested like Chinese boxes, with the abstract principles of each history occupying a level of temporal grammar corresponding to an order of predicate logic.

Because of the relation between self-awareness and temporal awareness, temporal stratification induces a stratification of self. What we have already described as the static intersect of momentary selves becomes a stratified relationship ... a terrace of temporal vantages conducing to long-term self-integration. As the self becomes stratified, the principles abstracted from higher orders of experience tend to be *objectivized* due to their generality, with science and philosophy among the results. Thus, the subjective and objective sides of reality – the self and the environment – tend to merge in a symmetric way. On one hand, the environment is absorbed by the self through experience, and the laws of nature are thereby abstracted; on the other hand, the self is projected onto the environment in such a way that it "selects" the laws of nature by analogy to its own internal laws. Either way, the core self tends to intersect with the environment as momentary selves are intersected within *it*. This brings the subjective and objective phases of reality – and time – into closer correspondence, blurring the distinction between them from an analytic standpoint.

As time grows more abstract, ways are sought to measure it, diagram it and analyze it numerically. This requires a universal depiction of space and time against which arbitrary processes can be differentially graphed and metered. Such a depiction was introduced by the Frenchman René Descartes in the first half of the 17th century. It was called *analytic geometry*, and it depicted time and the dimensions of space as straight, mutually perpendicular axes. In analytic geometry, any set of numerically-scaled space and time axes associated with any set of properties or attributes defines a *coordinate system* for assigning numbers to points, and simple processes appear as the graphs of algebraic functions. A few decades later, Newton and Leibniz independently discovered a new kind of mathematics, the *infinitesimal calculus*, by which to numerically quantify the rates of such processes. These innovations, which laid the foundations of modern science and engineering, suffice to this day in many practical contexts. Even though garden-variety analytic geometry was technically superseded by the Theory of Relativity - which was itself constructed on an analytic-geometric foundation - it gives a very close approximation of relativity in most situations.

Unfortunately, the conveniences of analytic geometry came at the price of *mind-body dualism*. This was Descartes' idea that the self, or "mind", was a nonphysical substance that could be left out of physical reasoning with impunity. For some purposes, this was true. But as we saw in the next-to-last paragraph, the *relationship* of mind to reality is not that simple. While the temporal grammar of physics determines the neural laws of cognition, cognitive grammar projects itself onto physical reality in such a way as to determine the form that physical grammar must assume. Because the *form* of physical grammar limits the *content* of physical grammar, this makes cognition a potential factor in determining the laws of nature. In principle, cognitive and physical grammars may influence each other symmetrically.

The symmetric influence of cognitive and physical grammars implies a directional symmetry of time. Although time is usually seen as a one-way street, it need not be; the mere fact that a street is marked "one way" does not stop it from being easily traveled in the unauthorized direction. Indeed, two-way time shows up in both quantum physics and relativity theory, the primary mainstays of modern physics. Thus, it is not physically warranted to say that cognition cannot influence the laws of physics because the laws of physics "precede cognition in time". If we look at the situation from the other direction, we can as easily say that cognition "precedes" the laws of physics in *reverse* time ... and point to the strange bidirectional laws of particle physics to justify our position. These laws are of such a nature that they can as well be called laws of *perception* as laws of *physics*.

Before we get to the final word on time, there is one more aspect of physical grammar that must be considered. Physical reasoning sometimes requires a distinction between two kinds of time: ordinary time and cosmic time. With respect to observations made at normal velocities, ordinary time behaves in a way described by Newtonian analytic geometry; at higher velocities, and in the presence of strong gravitational fields, it behaves according to Einstein's Special and General Theories of Relativity. But not long after Einstein formulated his General Theory, it was discovered that the universe, AKA spacetime, was *expanding*. Because cosmic expansion seems to imply that the universe began as a dimensionless point, the universe must have been *created*, and the creation event must have occurred on a higher level of time: cosmic time. Whereas ordinary time accommodates changes occurring within the spacetime manifold, this is obviously not so for the kind of time in which the manifold itself changes.

Now for the fly in the cosmological ointment. As we have seen, it is the nature of the cognitive self to formulate models incorporating ever-higher levels of change (or time). Obviously, the highest level of change is that characterizing the creation of reality. Prior to the moment of creation, the universe was *not* there; afterwards, the universe *was* there. This represents a sizable change indeed! Unfortunately, it also constitutes a sizable paradox. If the creation of reality was a real event, and if this event occurred in cosmic time, then cosmic time itself is real. But then cosmic time is an aspect of reality and can only have been created *with* reality. This implies that cosmic time, and in fact reality, must have created *themselves*!

The idea that the universe created itself brings a whole new meaning to bidirectional time, and thus to the idea that cognition may play a role in the creation of reality. As a self-creative mechanism for the universe is sought, it becomes apparent that cognition is the only process lending itself to plausible interpretation as a means of temporal feedback from present to past. Were cognition to play such a role, then in a literal sense, its most universal models of temporal reality would become identical to the reality being modeled. Time would become cognition, and space would become a system of geometric relations that evolves by distributed cognitive processing.

Here comes the surprise: such a model exists. Appropriately enough, it is called the *Cognitive-Theoretic Model of the Universe*, or CTMU for short (Langan, 2002). A cross between John Archibald Wheeler's Participatory Universe and the Stephen Hawking–James Hartle "imaginary time" theory of cosmology proposed in Hawking's phenomenal book *A Brief History of Time*, the CTMU resolves many of the most intractable paradoxes known to physical science while explaining recent data which indicate that the universe is expanding at an accelerating rate. Better yet, it bestows on human consciousness a level of meaning that was previously approached only by religion and mysticism. If it passes the test of time – and there are many good reasons to think that it will – then it will be the greatest step that humanity has yet taken towards a real understanding of its most (or least?) timeless mystery.

And so the circle closes. Time becomes a cosmogonic loop whereby the universe creates itself. The origin of our time concept, the self, becomes the origin of time itself. Our cognitive models of time become a model of time-as-cognition. And the languages of cognition and physics become one self-configuring, self-processing language of which time is the unified grammar. Talk about "time out of mind"!

And all this because of a little garden slug.

Which Came First?

Some people believe that children should be allowed to use their minds as freely and imaginatively as possible, without attention to the tedious laws of rationality. Others think that a child is never too young to get his or her first dose of logical and scientific reasoning. But in any case, a child with the intellectual maturity to ask a question like "which came first, the chicken or the egg?" is probably ready for a valuable lesson in logic and biology ... more of a lesson, perhaps, than many of us are ready to give. This little essay aims to change all that, and thereby protect you and your pint-size inquisitors from the perils of ignorance (and specifically, being recognized as an incurable case thereof!).

The question "which came first, the chicken or the egg?" looks at first glance like a matter of straightforward repro-ductive biology. But before we can even begin to answer this question, we must define our terms. So actually, it is a classic case of semantic ambiguity ... a problem of meaning and interpretation. Specifically, while the term "chicken" is biologically unambiguous – we all know what a chicken looks, sounds and tastes like – the term "egg" is somewhat more general and is therefore a possible source of ambiguity. Do we mean (1) just any egg, or (2) a *chicken* egg? And if we're talking about a chicken egg, then is a "chicken egg" (2a) an egg laid by a chicken, (2b) an egg containing a chicken, or (2c) both? Reformulating the question to reflect each possible meaning of "egg" leads to four distinct versions of the chicken-or-egg question:

1. Which came first, the chicken or (just any old) egg?

2a.   Which came first, the chicken or an egg *laid by* a chicken?

2b.   Which came first, the chicken or an egg *containing* a chicken?

2c.   Which came first, the chicken, or an egg laid by *and* containing a chicken?

Contrary to popular belief, there is indeed a definite answer to each of these questions. Specifically, the answers are: (1) The egg. (2a) The chicken. (2b) The egg. (2c) The chicken. Given some knowledge of logic and biology, these answers are not hard to verify. To get this show on – or should that be across? – the road, let's go through them in order.

First, consider question 1: which came first, the chicken or (just any old) egg? This question is answered "the egg" because species that lay eggs have been around a lot longer than modern chickens. For example, we have plenty of fossil evidence that dinosaurs laid eggs from which baby dinosaurs hatched, and dinosaurs predate chickens by millions of years. Indeed, a growing body of research indicates that dinosaurs were among the biological *ancestors* of chickens!

Now let's look at question 2a: which came first, the chicken or an egg *laid by* a chicken? The answer to this question is "the chicken" on semantic grounds alone. That is, if a chicken egg must be laid by a chicken, then before a chicken egg can exist, there must *by definition* be a chicken around to lay it. And question 2c – which came first, the chicken or an egg laid by *and* containing a chicken? – is answered the same way on the same grounds; logically, the fact that a chicken egg must be laid by a chicken precedes and therefore "dominates" the (biologically subsequent) requirement that it contain a chicken. So whereas we needed paleozoological evidence to answer question 1, questions 2a and 2c require practically no biological knowledge at all!

Having saved the best for last, let us finally consider the most interesting version, 2b: which came first, the chicken or an egg *containing* a chicken? This version is interesting because an egg containing a chicken might have been laid by a chicken *or* a non-chicken, which of course affects the answer. Thanks to modern genetic science, we can now be sure that the egg came first. This is because reproductive mutations separating a new species from its progenitor generally occur in reproductive rather than somatic DNA and are thus expressed in differences between successive generations, but not in the parent organisms themselves. While the *somatic* (body) cells of the parents – e.g. wing cells, drumstick cells and wishbone cells – usually contain only the DNA with which they were conceived, *germ* (reproductive) cells like ova and spermatozoa contain non-somatic DNA that may have been changed before or during mating by accidental deletion, insertion, substitution, duplication or translocation of nucleotide sequences. This is what causes the mutation that results in the new species.

Where an animal qualifies as a member of a given species only if its somatic DNA (as opposed to its reproductive DNA) conforms to the genotype of the species, the parents of the first member of a new species are not members of that new species. At the same time, all the biological evidence says that the ancestors of modern chickens were already oviparous or egg-laying ... that a male and a female member of the ancestral species of the modern chicken, call this species "protochicken", mated with each other and created an egg. (Could the first chicken have evolved from a viviparous or live-bearing species, and after being born alive, have started laying eggs? All the biological evidence says "no".) But because their act of mating involved a shuffling of reproductive genes that were not expressed in the body of either parent – if they *had* been expressed there, the parents would themselves have been members of the new species – the fetus inside the egg was not like them. Instead, it was a mutant ... a modern chicken!

Only two loose ends remain: the "gradual" and "sudden" extremes of the evolutionary spectrum. These extremes are *evolutionary gradualism* – Darwin's original slow-paced timetable for natural selection – and *punctuated evolution*, as advocated more recently by evolutionary theorists including the controversial Stephen J. Gould.

Gradualism says that mutations are biologically random, but subject to a selection process determined by environmental (external) conditions to which species must *adapt* over the course of many generations. Taken to the limit, it implies either that each minor mutation that occurs during the evolutionary change of one species into another is random and independent of any other mutation, in which case a useful combination of mutations is highly improbable, or that each individual mutation confers a selective advantage on the mutant ... that every evolutionary advantage of a new species over its precursor decomposes into smaller advantages combined in a more or less linear way. Unfortunately, this makes it almost impossible to explain complex biological structures that do not break down into smaller structures useful in their own right ... structures like bacterial cilia and flagella, and even the human eye.

The hypothetical gradualistic evolution of one species into another via mutations accumulated over many generations leads to the following question: when does the quality and quantity of mutations justify a distinction between "species" ... when does a protochicken become a chicken? It's a good question, but our chicken-or-egg answers remain valid no matter how we answer it.

At the other extreme, evolution sometimes appears to progress by leaps and bounds, moving directly from the old to the new in "punctuated" fashion. And to complicate matters, this sometimes seems to happen across the board, affecting many species at once. The most oft-cited example of punctuated evolution is the *Cambrian Explosion*. Whereas sedimentary rocks that formed more than about 600 million years ago are poor in fossils of multicellular organisms, slightly younger rocks contain a profusion of such fossils conforming to many different structural templates. The duration of the so-called "explosion", a mere geological eyeblink of no more than 10 million years or so, is inconsistent with gradualism;

new organs and appendages must have been popping out faster than the environment alone could have selected them from a field of random mutations. Clearly, the sudden appearance of a new appendage would leave little doubt about the evolutionary demarcation of ancestral and descendant species.

But the kind of punctuated evolution that occurs between generations is not the end of the line in sheer biological acceleration. Sometimes, an evolutionary change seems to occur within the lifespan of a single organism! For example, in the spirit of "ontogeny recapitulates phylogeny", insect metamorphosis almost seems to hint at an evolutionary process in which an ancient grub or caterpillar underwent a sudden transformation to something with wings and an exoskeleton ... or alternatively, in which a hard-shelled flying bug suddenly gave birth to an egg containing a soft and wormy larva. While that's not what really happened – as is so often the case, the truth lies somewhere in the middle – what occurred was just as marvelous and just as punctuated.

What seems to have happened was this. Due to a reproductive mutation, a whole sequence of evolutionary changes originally expressed in the fetal development of an ancestral arthropod, and originally recapitulated within the womb and egg it inhabited, were suddenly exposed to the environment, or at least to the hive, in a case of "ovum interruptus". A fetal stage of morphogenesis that formerly occurred within womb and egg was interrupted when the egg hatched "prematurely", making the soft fetus into an equally soft larva and giving it a valuable opportunity to seek crucial nourishment from external sources before being enclosed in a *pupa*, a second egg-like casing from which it later hatched again in its final exoskeletal form. So metamorphosis turns out to be a case of biological common sense, providing the fetus-cum-larva with an opportunity to acquire the nourishment required for the energy-consuming leap into adulthood.

Does this affect our answer to the chicken-or-egg question? Not really. For even where the life cycle of an organism includes distinct morphological stages, the DNA of egg-laying insects does not change after conception. And since it is reproductive and not somatic DNA modification that distinguishes one species from the next in line, our answers stand firm. (Of course, this says nothing of science fiction movies in which something bizarre and insidious causes runaway mutations in the somatic DNA of hapless humans, causing them to evolve into monsters before our very eyes! Such humans have either undergone a random or radiation-induced "meta-mutation" whereby their genetic code suddenly rearranged itself to incorporate a self-modification routine that is executed somatically, within their own cells, or they are the victims of a space virus which inserted such a routine into their DNA for its own nefarious purposes.)

OK ... perhaps there's yet another loose end. Asking which of two things came first implies that time flows in a straight line from past to future (those are the "loose ends"). But what if time were to flow in either direction, or even to loop around, flowing in what amounts to a circle? No more loose ends. In fact, loops have no ends at all! But in this case, the answer depends on whether we're on the forward or reverse side of the loop, heading towards the future or the past. Another way to formulate this question: does the cause lead to the effect, or is there a sense in which the effect leads to the cause? Suffice it to say that no matter which way we choose to go, the original answers to the four versions (1, 2a, 2b and 2c) of the chicken-or-egg question are all affected the same way. They are either all unchanged or all reversed, with no additional ambiguity save that pertaining to the direction of time (not a problem for most non-physicists and non-cosmologists).

Now that we've tied up every last loose end, what about the most important question of all, namely what to tell a curious child? The answer: take your pick of versions. Some kids will prefer the dinosaur angle of version 1; some kids will prefer the "birds and bees" reproductive biology lesson of version 2b. In my opinion, if we limit ourselves to one version only, the most valuable explanation is probably that of 2b; but due to its relative complexity, a younger child can probably derive greater benefit from a T. Rex-versus-Triceratops embellishment of version 1. To exhaust the golden opportunities for logical and scientific instruction, one should of course answer all four versions. But no matter which way you go, make sure the child knows exactly which version(s) of the question you're answering. If you leave out the one he or she had in mind, you'll no doubt be egged on until it gets answered!

Of Trees, Quads and God

Ever hear this old Ronald Knox limerick about a lonely tree?

> There was a young man who said, "God
> Must think it exceedingly odd
>   If he finds that this tree
>   Continues to be
> When there's no one about in the Quad."

REPLY

> Dear Sir, Your astonishment's odd:
> I am always about in the Quad.
>   And that's why the tree
>   Will continue to be
> Since observed by, Yours faithfully, God.

No? Then perhaps you've heard the old koan-like question that seems to be every schoolchild's introduction to philosophy (it's still about a lonely tree, but at least this one is doing something): "If a tree falls in the forest and no one is there to hear it, does it make a sound?"

No, you say again? Then for the consolation prize, maybe you'd like to guess what the limerick and the question have in common.

The answer is twofold. They're both about the empirical philosophy of the celebrated 18th century philosopher Bishop George Berkeley. (That's right – Berkeley was a bishop as well as a philosopher. How else could God have gotten into a philosopher's limerick? Oh, yes . . . Knox was a cleric too!) And they're both about the relationship between reality and perception, or more generally, the relationship between reality and mind.

As with most philosophers, the nature of reality was something that preoccupied Berkeley. The nature of reality ... now, there's a difficult topic. The first thing we notice about reality is that it's everywhere. And the next thing we notice about it is that because it's everywhere, there's nothing around to contrast it with or compare it to in order to define it. There are always dreams, fantasies and illusions, of course, but what are they? And if we don't know what *they* are, then how can we use them to define reality?

The problem gets worse. An understanding of reality as the medium of existence is necessary for understanding anything that exists. We're parts of reality. So if we don't know what reality is, how do we know what *we* are? And if we don't know what we are, then how do we know what anything else is? Indeed, how do we know anything at all? (I'm sorry to say that this is not a joke, but a sad reality.)

Science doesn't help. When we use science, all we're doing is using various parts of reality to define other parts, not defining reality with respect to its complement. We can't just point to physical reality and say, "there it is ... that's what reality consists of!" while banging our knuckles or heads against a massive object, e.g. a table or wall, to drive home the sheer solidity of our conviction. For physical reality is not a stand-alone proposition; it requires universal rules in order to exist and maintain its consistency. And from a logical standpoint, those rules are more than merely physical.

Let's go back to every schoolchild's introduction to philosophy for a moment. "If a tree falls in the forest and no one is there to hear it, does it make a sound?" It is no accident that people have come to regard this as a western version of "what is the sound of one hand clapping?", for both can be reduced to the notion of unrequited duality.

In the case of one hand clapping, the duality is the concept of (two-handed) clapping, and the missing part of the duality is the other (non-clapping) hand, which is either absent or motionless depending on the point you want to make. In the case of the sound made by the tree falling in the forest, the duality is the concept of a sound, and the missing part is the listener. For in contrast to the objective physical disturbance called a "sound wave", a sound is a *perception* that requires both an object to make it and a subject to hear it.

The lesson is clear: when it comes to perception, it takes two to tango. Perception is a duality involving both object and subject; for every perception, there is something perceived and someone who perceives it. But here the clarity ends, for the lesson has more than one possible interpretation. In fact, there are two, each one predicated on a distinct hypothetical relationship between perception and reality.

The first of these relational hypotheses goes like this: perception and reality are separate. Perhaps the foremost exponent of this viewpoint was the French mercenary, philosopher and mathematician René Descartes (1596-1650). At this point, we need to know just two things about Descartes, the first being that he was a *rationalist*. Rationalists believe that the most basic concepts in terms of which we understand the world – e.g. self and causality – are known intuitively rather than through experience. Descartes held that we can deduce truths with absolute certainty from such "innate ideas" in the same way that theorems are deduced from axioms in geometry. In fact, rationalists see mathematical demonstration as the perfect means of establishing truth, and thus as a general model for the pursuit of knowledge.

The second thing we need to know about Descartes is that his philosophy was dualistic, positing an absolute separation between mind and matter ... and specifically, the human mind and body. To put it another way, Descartes said that reality consists of two independent substances, mind and matter. Both are real, Descartes assured us, but never the twain shall meet except through the act of perception, which must itself have a dual nature in order to bridge the gap. (In contrast to *dualism*, which reduces reality to two essential, irreducible substances, *pluralism* reduces it to many and *monism* reduces it to just one. The problem with any -ism other than monism, however, is that one gets stuck trying to explain the composition of the medium in which the various essential substances are related to each other.)

The second relational hypothesis is that perception and reality are intimately related. The first philosopher usually associated with this viewpoint was the Englishman John Locke (1632-1704). Locke argued against the rationalist belief in innate ideas, holding that the mind is a *tabula rasa* or "blank slate" on which all knowledge is imprinted by experience. He distinguished primary objective qualities like number, extension and solidity, which mechanically affect the sense organs through perception, from secondary subjective qualities like color, smell and sound, which are produced by the direct impact of the world on the sense organs. Once past the sense organs, Locke theorized, these secondary experiential qualities combined to form ideas that mirror reality and constitute the basis of science.

But what kind of science? Although Locke believed that we know the world only through experience, he also believed in the existence of a world apart from the mind, with perception and experience mediating between the mind and the world around it. It thus seems that Locke's apple fell not too far from Descartes' tree after all. For his theory of primary and secondary qualities, whereby the mind knows only secondhand experiences impressed upon it by perception, implies that scientific knowledge is itself a secondhand affair ... that the true essences of physical objects cannot be scientifically known. So Locke agreed with Descartes not only about mind–body duality – that the conceptual, subjective world of the mind is forever separate from the concrete, objective world it perceives – but that mathematics is the only route to certainty.

So far, the only real difference between Descartes and Locke is ... well, not much. Descartes says that the mind possesses innate knowledge; Locke says that the mind is a blank slate on which reality leaves its imprint. But in the final analysis, the intuition-versus-*tabula rasa* distinction turns out not to make a lot of difference. For Descartes and Locke are both dualists, and their respective solutions of the tree-in-the-quad problem are exactly the same: since the material existence of trees is independent of perception, they exist whether or not anyone is watching them. This agreement is quite strange in view of the fact that Descartes and Locke are respectively considered to be the founders of *rationalism* and *empiricism*, two opposing philosophies about the source of human knowledge. So where do these philosophies diverge?

Enter George "What-you-see-is-what-you-get" Berkeley (1685-1753), an Anglo-Irish philosopher and clergyman who went Locke one better. Whereas Locke had allowed the independent existence of matter, Berkeley held that reality and perception are one and the same, and thus that matter cannot exist without perception. (In the intellectual style of the day, he dressed his thesis up in Latin: *esse est percipi*, "to be is to be perceived.") Technically, this made him an adherent of *idealism*, a strain of philosophy which holds that nothing exists apart from minds and their contents. In contrast to the mind-body dualism of Descartes, Berkeley's perceptual monism reduced reality to a single "substance", perception.

Whereas Locke had believed that real objects possess their own innate qualities along with mental qualities stimulated by perception, Berkeley held that all qualities are mental or ideal in nature. But he also acknowledged a key distinction: whereas ideas are mutable and evanescent, material objects are stable and persistent. From this, he reasoned that the mind on which material objects depend must be divine rather than human. That is, from the common-sense notion that physical objects exist even when no one perceives them, Berkeley inferred that the Official Perceiver of trees and other objects must be God Himself. Where Locke's philosophy had opened the epistemological door to the demons of skepticism and atheism,

Berkeley aimed to close it and thereby restore faith in God.

At this point, we should note that the God-in-the-quad answer to the tree-in-the-quad question is in some ways an oversimplification. In fact, Berkeley would have said that the material quad does not exist at all except as an archetype in God's mind, God's own subjective description of the quad's physical appearance. According to Berkeley, people who enter the quad will have the appropriate mental experiences, i.e. will "perceive" the quad, only because these experiences are produced by reference to God's own archetype. Just as a musician produces music by reference to the composer's musical score, we perceive quads by referring to the contents of the Mind of God; our perception follows God's cognition. To this extent, Berkeley's perceptual monism is *cognitive* monism.

If Berkeley's reality-equals-perception thesis seems radical, then watch out for the Scottish philosopher and historian David Hume (1711-76). Hume carried the empiricism of Locke and Berkeley to the logical extreme of *radical skepticism*, repudiating the possibility of certain knowledge. According to Hume, the mind is nothing but a series of sensations, and causality is merely an illusion that happens when one impression follows another. Even though cause precedes effect, says Hume, there is no proof that the cause is responsible for the effect's occurrence. Unfortunately, because Hume also disagreed with Berkeley on the subject of God and flatly rejected theology, he took the tree-in-the-quad problem out of God's perceptual lap and put it back in man's (not an entirely fortuitous move, given the increasing prevalence of attention deficit disorder).

The vulnerability of Hume's reality to ADD is not the only problem associated with his philosophy. Hume is also credited with another problem, the so-called *problem of induction*: how do human beings form beliefs about unobserved matters of fact, and are these beliefs justified? That is, do our powers of reasoning permit us to form valid conclusions about parts of nature we have not observed? The bearing of this problem on that of the tree-in-the-quad is obvious: in principle, a strong constructive solution for the problem of induction would let us determine the existence of any tree anywhere from our perception of any subset of trees. If human reasoning were sufficiently powerful, and human powers of generalization sufficiently strong, then to perceive any subset of trees would be as good as perceiving them all. In effect, human cognition (and not divine) would suffice to relieve perception of much of its ontological responsibility.

But that would be optimistic, and Hume was not an optimist. Indeed, his solution to the problem of induction was downright gloomy. First, he defined induction as the construction of a general theory from limited data by applying a principle asserting the uniformity of nature. That is, induction generalizes from the part to the whole on the assumption that nature is everywhere the same. From this it followed that all beliefs about unobserved facts are derived by induction from experience. But while Hume considered the inductive schema (pattern of reasoning) logically valid, he denied the validity of the uniformity premise. For while the validity of the premise can only be established by induction, every inductive argument necessarily employs it. Since the premise is "circular" or self-justifying, said Hume, it cannot be proven.

After Hume did his bit, things looked bad indeed for any tree unlucky enough to be in an empty quad; neither God nor induction could philosophically warrant its existence. But even as the gloom of radical skepticism cast its pall over much of Europe, all was not lost. For if Hume was the philosophical Little Engine That Could, he and his followers were about to learn the meaning of Kant.

Immanuel Kant (1724-1804) was a German philosopher who complained of being awakened from his "dogmatic slumber" by the Little Engine's whistle, a shock which prompted him to synthesize the skepticism of Hume with the rationalism of Descartes' fellow rationalist Gottfried Wilhelm von Leibniz. Kant's central thesis was this: we can know objective reality only insofar as it conforms to the structure of our minds.

Beyond this point, Kant deemed reality unknowable. Kant called knowable objects of experience *phenomena*, and the unknowable objects underlying these phenomena *noumena* or "things-in-themselves" (think "objects independent of perception"). By definition, noumena are immune to affirmation, denial or scientific confirmation. Unfortunately, there is a problem with the Kantian relationship between phenomena and noumena: it is bedeviled by a particularly troublesome form of dualism that resists transformation into a unified (monic) explanation of reality. Whereas Descartes asserts that mind and matter occupy a divinely-mandated similarity relationship, Kant denies that the parallel relationship between phenomena and noumena can be known at all, even to the extent of calling it a "similarity relationship". From this follows some bad news: noumenal trees are untouchable by phenomenal perception. But there is some good news as well: phenomenal trees must conform to the structure of our minds. In principle, this yields a solution to the problem of induction with respect to phenomenal reality.

Although it may seem hard to believe, this brings us right up to the present in terms of "metaphysics", or our knowledge of deep reality. Indeed, since Kant's linkage between phenomenal reality and the structure of our minds invites further exploration, it propels us towards the future. Even now, science struggles in vain with the problem of induction, waiting for philosophy to tell it how to construct a general theory of reality from the limited data accessible to its instruments; floundering in a confusing welter of dualism, rationalism and empiricism, it cries out for a metaphysical resolution. But analytic philosophy, long ago cowed by the brilliant successes of its scientific offspring, remains preoccupied with emulating the hard sciences, and thus finds little room for metaphysical thought. As each side looks vainly to the other for guidance, it sees only its own shadow.

But the tree-in-the-quad saga is not yet over. Using ideas from each of the above philosophers along with some newer concepts, it is possible to synthesize a new mind-matter, mind-body connection that leaves reality neither irrevocably split, nor hanging in the ontological limbo of a quad at once atheistic, noumenal and empty. Look to the future. For when science and philosophy remarry at last, their progeny will populate and enrich our intellectual world.

The Pros and Cons of "Machine Intelligence"

If you want to be intelligent, you have to be smart about it. And the first thing you need to know about intelligence is that it comes in two varieties: natural and artificial. Let's start with the shallow, artificial kind and save the deep stuff for later. (Then let's show that the two cannot be objectively distinguished and pretend they're the same.)

AI, oh magical acronym! Artificial Intelligence, perhaps the hottest topic of the digital era, has captivated the imaginations of computer scientists and screenwriters since the days of vacuum tubes and punch cards. But as any star buzzword should know, it's a long fall from the top, and being overhyped is little better than not being hyped at all. AI, having failed repeatedly to emerge on schedule, now finds itself with a bad record, a bad name, and increasingly bad credit at the Bank of Big Expectations (in fact, the alternate title for this piece was "The Gurus of AI – Pros or Cons?").

No big surprise, really. It was all right there in the name. "Artificial" and "intelligence" go together like *jumbo* and *shrimp*, *communist* and *party*, or *educational* and *television*. Indeed, insofar as *artificial* is nothing but an antonym of *real*, AI seems to have shot itself point-blank in the foot with Webster's Collegiate Dictionary. No wonder, then, that it seems all but destined to go the way of genuine *pleather*, real imitation fur and bona fide faux pearls. As it now stands, AI is the stuff of late-night TV ... of hardcore sci-fi and breathless blurbs for various direct-marketed techno-toys.

However, there are a couple of new and disturbing trends on the horizon. In fact, they started at the horizon some time ago and have since gotten considerably closer. Do they involve startling breakthroughs in computer science? Well, yes and no. They *do* involve computers. But the "science" has at least as much to do with biology – or as they say in the AI biz, "wetware" – as with hardware and software, and it opens up a number of disturbing possibilities reminiscent of movies like *Colossus: The Forbin Project*, *Demon Seed*, *War Games*, *Terminator* and *The Matrix*. Suffice it to say that if you still take solace from the trite belief that "computers can't do anything we humans don't program them to do!", you need to ... well, re–compute your position.

But before we go there, let's answer the obvious question: how did it all begin? That's easy – it began with Alan Turing. The subject of a play called *Breaking The Code* – he was famous for cracking Germany's "uncrackable" Enigma code in WW2 – Turing was a British mathematician whose ideas sowed the seeds of modern computer science. No sooner had scientists wishfully added electronic computers to the List of Neat Things We Want for Christmas, than their friends the mathematicians began to use abstract models to explore their capabilities. As the world waited for a real computer to be built, Turing's *universal machine* became the abstract model computer of choice. A harbinger of disappointments to come, Turing used it to show that there are problems that no computer will ever be able to solve (in effect, Turing mathematically fed a symbolic universal machine to itself and then stepped back to avoid the flying nuts–and–bolts symbols).

Not one to give up, Turing nevertheless went on to become the world's first AI theorist. First, he reasoned that a computer would some day become powerful enough to duplicate some of the functions of the human mind. Would this make the computer intelligent? To answer this question would require a test, but of what kind? Since subjective attributes like intelligence do not readily lend themselves to the scientific method, the test should measure the objective correlates of intelligence rather than intelligence itself. But against what scale? Since people introspectively know how it feels to be intelligent, and know intelligence when they encounter it in others, human judgment should serve as the scale. So the best test, reasoned Turing, would be to put a computer and a person on opposite sides of an opaque partition and let them interact, e.g. engage in a written dialogue. If the person is fooled into thinking that another person is behind the partition, then the computer passes the *Turing Test* for artificial intelligence.

Unfortunately, a machine that fools a human proves itself no more than a convincing fake. After all, the computer can do nothing but what it is programmed to do ... or can it? Granted, a computer is mechanical. But human beings can themselves be described as biomechanical systems. Granted, a computer is deterministically programmed and therefore devoid of free will. But there remains a philosophical controversy over the possession of free will by humans, whose own "programming" involves a mixture of genetics and environmental exposure over which they arguably have little control. In fact, Turing even described abstract machines capable of making intelligent guesses, which amounts to a form of free will and obscures the distinction completely. So where is the functional difference between computers and people? The superficiality of the Turing Test – its failure to probe beneath surface appearances in search of the "true essence" of intelligence, human or otherwise – reflects the difficulty of pinning down this distinction, at least for a mathematician.

The bottom line: our best working definition of intelligence is "problem-solving ability". But then the meaning of *intelligence* devolves to that of *problem*, and where a "problem" is whatever you want it to be, intelligence is whatever you want it to be as well. Which, of course, recreates the original problem, namely how to find a meaningful definition of intelligence. This takes us right back to the Turing Test, which – if we sensibly go along with Turing regarding the limitations of the scientific method with respect to subjective predicates like intelligence –is an optimal test of intelligence in man *or* machine. After all, when one person sits behind a partition and gives another person an IQ test, this is merely a quantitative refinement of the Turing Test involving no *a priori* distinction between a human being and a test-taking computer program. This means that when it comes to intelligence, we might as well talk about it in terms of machines as human beings. So let's just pick up where Turing left off.

Not too long after Turing invented his eponymous abstract model of a computer, real mechanical computers had been built and were ready to be put to the Turing Test for machine intelligence. When programmers first considered ways of doing this, it occurred to them that there were a couple of obvious methods at their disposal. They could program a computer to play a game against a human and either beat the human or come close to it. Or they could program a computer to convincingly answer a series of questions ordinarily posed to a human expert like a doctor or a lawyer. Either way, they reasoned, a human participant behind a partition would have a hard time figuring out that he was being bamboozled by a bag of hot circuits. And thus originated two of the main currents in AI, gaming programs and *expert systems*.

The most famous gaming program of all time is *Deep Blue*, the wood-pushing automaton that beat World Chess Champion Garry Kasparov in 3.5 out of 6 games in May, 1997 (in a draw, each player gets ½ game). Billed by *Newsweek* as "The Brain's Last Stand", it was ballyhooed as a huge victory for AI. Unfortunately, if there was ever a Turing-style partition between the players, it was anything but opaque. In response to each of Kasparov's moves, the machine was known to be rapidly executing thousands upon thousands of lines of code containing cumulative "if ... then" statements, something of which a human mind would be incapable even if it seemed like a good idea. Partition or not, it was all too clear that the combination of heuristics and brute force employed by Deep Blue was not what most of us really mean by "intelligence".

What about expert systems? To build an expert system, a "knowledge engineer" interviews experts in a given field and tries to collect their knowledge in a computer program designed to answer questions or perform one or more domain-specific tasks. Unfortunately, because the operations that the computer is required to perform are not always feasible, this doesn't always work. In recent times, expert systems designers have met with limited success. But there are two problems. First, the computer is clearly not "thinking"; it is merely storing, sorting and relaying the insights of human experts. Second, as soon as the program's human interlocutor transgresses the bounds of its narrow range of borrowed "expertise", it typically starts making stupid errors that give it away.

These problems apply not just to specific AI programs and the machines that execute them. They apply to the entire AI strategy including gaming programs, expert systems, mathematical theorem-proving programs, natural language parsers, so-called "intelligent agents" and other conventional automated procedures designed to mimic human intellectual processes. Once this became obvious, the search began for alternative approaches. Among the possibilities, two stood out. The first, now referred to as *connectionism*, was to directly simulate the human brain on the intercellular level. The second, called by suggestive names like *genetic algorithms* and *evolutionary programming*, was an idea that had long been talked about, but seemed so improbable and outrageous that few took it seriously: instead of mimicking the output of biological systems, programmers would attempt to electronically recreate them.

Connectionism aims to duplicate human intellectual abilities using the brain's simplified model of its own structure: the artificial neural network. Just as a brain consists of neurons connected by synapses, a neural network consists of artificial neurons called "neurodes" and their "synaptic" interconnections. To each connection is assigned a strength or "weight". The pattern of synaptic weights is the network's "program" ... the informational construct according to which input is converted to output. However, the weighting pattern is not the *whole* program. The neural net also incorporates a higher-level program called a *learning function* that adjusts synaptic weights according to input. The learning function tells the network how to do what the brain does effortlessly, but computers can do only badly if at all: learn from experience. Already, neural nets quickly but fallibly learn such tasks as facial recognition, rudimentary language processing and predicting the stock market.

Notice what this does to the idea that "computers can only do what we program them to do". The brainlike computer called a neural net is equipped with a higher-level program that lets it *program itself*. Feel things starting to get out of control yet? If so, then get ready for another eye-opener. For according to the genetic programmers, it simply won't do to build lifelike computers when you can do what Mother Nature did: get them to build themselves by the process of evolution.

First, the genetic programmers create a random population of computer programs to perform a given task or set of tasks. Each program is measured against a "fitness criterion" by which the degree of correctness of its output may be determined. A "selection principle" then rewards fitter programs with a survival advantage – that is, a higher probability of survival – and penalizes the less fit, making them more likely to die out. As in nature, survivors have the opportunity to "breed", in the course of which they can mutate and combine to form new programs that inherit their traits. After many generations, evolution produces programs that have the highest possible level of fitness ... programs that can perform the intended set of tasks (almost) perfectly, thus filling the available niche in their electronic ecosystem. (This seldom holds true when new tasks are added, but what did you expect?) Evolution triumphs again.

It would be hard to overestimate the profundity of these trends. In adopting genetic and connectionist viewpoints, AI intersects with biology on multiple scales. It thus promises to outdo humanity itself, which – let's face it – has put meaningful adaptive pressure, and thus evolution, on hold by suspending the law of natural selection. As it stands, a human with low fitness can apply a series of temporary medical patches to whatever ails him or her and reproduce like a rabbit anyway, intelligence notwithstanding. Not so for genetic programs, which we subject to ruthless adaptative pressure to serve us.

The bad news: connectionism and genetic programming still have a very long way to go. Both are resource-intensive, requiring huge parallel processors to work up to capacity, and their theories are still relatively primitive. Moreover, the opaque panel in the Turing Test is essentially the same divider used by Descartes, in his doctrine of Cartesian Dualism, to separate mind from matter and sever the mind–body connection in the name of science. Thus, like Cartesian dualism itself, the Turing Test offers no insight to the intrinsic nature of intelligence; in the current state of philosophy, all we can say is that "intelligence is as intelligence does".

The good news: there is a way out. But it involves a shift from Cartesian dualism to cognitive monism and the concept of an "intelligent universe", according to which generalized intelligence becomes a universal property of which our minds are just localized examples (yes, that's what it ultimately takes to restore the mind–body connection). One thing's for sure: the future will be as interesting as the theories of AI and biology put together, and it is a future for which we must prepare. Because we desperately need to understand the machines we will be creating and how they relate to us, hiding behind our Cartesian panel is no longer a viable option. Philosophically, we need to step into the New Millennium, and fast.

Meanwhile, no matter what happens – no matter what the danger that mankind will fall under the domination of a tyrannical AI monster like those in the movies mentioned above – we can take solace in one little fact: the way things are going in our public schools, it is virtually certain that no self-respecting machine will ever pass the Turing Test. You see, such a machine will immediately give itself away by its use of proper grammar.

In Ethics, Not Everything is Relative

After the events of 9-11, destructive and heroic, it seems like a good time to discuss ethics and moral relativism. We all know the meaning of ethics; ethics are what tell human beings how to do the right thing by each other. Unfortunately, this can be a very complex calculation, and that's where moral relativism enters the picture.

To understand moral relativism, consider asking many people the following question: "Was the World Trade Center disaster morally wrong?" In New York City and across the rest of the US, this question would be sure to draw an overwhelming number of affirmative responses. But if one were to ask this question in the streets of an enemy nation of the US, the answers might be very different. One might instead hear a series of blame-the-victims tirades about how US meddling and/or non-meddling in the affairs of other sovereign nations entitles those nations to lash out violently against their "oppressors" (us).

In other words, we have two points of view, one associated with the victims of the tragedy and the other with its actual or would-be perpetrators. Each of these viewpoints is clearly the opposite of the other, as reflected in "yes" and "no" answers to the same question. It would seem to follow that only one can be "moral" or "ethical" ... that one side should be able to prove itself "right", and the other should have to admit being "wrong".

However, we know from practical experience that such agreements can be very elusive. More often than not, each side in a dispute claims the moral high ground. This, of course, tends to rob of its meaning the concept of ethical or moral correctness. If it were simultaneously true that the lightest shade is white and the lightest shade is black, then the "lightness" attribute would have no power to distinguish one shade from another, and this would correspond to ambiguity in the meanings of "white" and "black". The ethical analogue of this dilemma involves ambiguity in the meanings of "good" and "evil", and "right" and "wrong".

How is this ethical dilemma to be solved? One way would be to provide an absolute definition of terms like good, evil, right and wrong, spelling out the good-evil / right-wrong distinction in such a way that it could be straightforwardly applied in any context to identify the best course of action. Attempts to define absolute good include the Ten Commandments, which consist of absolute instructions to be obeyed unconditionally by good people; the US Bill of Rights, a list of absolute freedoms to be unconditionally respected by good citizens and good governments; and the Golden Rule, a sophisticated rolling of many ethical principles into one.

But ethical absolutism is not without its difficulties. To take a simple if unpleasant example, suppose that the child of a penniless man is suffering from a terrible but curable disease, that the man's every attempt to get money to pay for the very expensive cure has failed, and that the manufacturer of the cure has ignored his every plea for mercy. Now suppose that the man knows where the cure is stored in quantity, and that he has a good chance of stealing a dose without detection. Should he be deterred from doing so by the fact that theft is wrong, given that it would also be wrong to let his innocent child die?

If we examine this situation closely, we can discern the involvement of at least three distinct viewpoints or "ethical frames". The first is that of the man and his child, whose joint purpose is to save the child's life. The next is that of the manufacturer of the cure, whose purpose is to get a maximum (or perhaps just a fair) return on his investment in R&D and production. And the third frame, which contains the first two, is an overall context with respect to which the absolute morality of "thou shalt not steal" has putatively been determined, but which nevertheless lacks any absolute proscription against letting innocent children die for their poverty.

Such examples seem to imply that no finite set of specific moral principles suffices to determine ethical behavior in a real world characterized by endless complications. This has led to an even less productive way of approaching ethical dilemmas, namely moral relativism. A moral relativist takes the following position: it is useless to speculate about the moral laws of an overall context that can never be fully known. Because the right-wrong distinction thus depends on the specific viewpoints of those who apply it, we can do no better than consider each frame independently, reformulating the distinction when switching from one frame to the other.

This putative independence of ethical frames tends to render them incommensurable, impeding the formation of common goals and cooperation to achieve them. This restricts the moral relativist to the default "common goal" of mutual tolerance. But where mere tolerance is sufficient, or where at least one viewpoint is defined precisely by its intolerance, this can be unproductive, and the relativist is powerless to fix the problem. For while fixing the problem would require either the imposition of a common ethic or a judgment against intolerance, moral relativism lacks an ethical basis for taking such measures or validating such judgments.

For example, consider the problem of constructing an extended context in which the Western and Islamic worlds can peacefully coexist. One side believes in freedom, capitalism and the separation of church and state; the other believes in various blends of feudalism, theocracy and plutocracy. One has given its citizens the world's highest average quality of life; the other has concentrated its considerable wealth in the hands of an incredibly opulent ruling class that is perfectly happy to let the impoverished masses blame outsiders for their problems. One treats even its criminals with compassion; the other summarily plucks out eyes and lops off body parts from hands to heads.

And the differences go on. One side regards women as full and equal citizens; the other regards them as something less. One allows itself to be criticized by its own citizens and shapes its policies according to their will; the other appoints external scapegoats for all of its problems and lashes out at them instead of cleaning up its own political domicile. One is a diverse family of immigrants that generously opens its doors to the world with a promise of equal opportunity; the other belongs to a set of warring groups characterized by millennia of bloodshed and turmoil, unfair distribution of resources, and annihilative creeds encouraging preferred groups to subject other groups to physical, psychological and economic violence "in the name of God".

Such examples point to the main weakness of moral relativism: in failing to distinguish between absolute right and wrong, it renders itself unable to deal equitably with situations in which one side is more right than another. It balances the pain of the victim against the pleasure of the victimizer, the agony of a murdered child against the dark ecstasy of the fiend who murders her. Indeed, it places the very angels of Heaven and devils of Hell on an equal footing; confronted by angels pleading for brotherly love and devils bent on human pain and misery, the pure moral relativist would have to juggle the benefits of brotherly love with those of demonic torment. (After all, millions of sadistic, bloodthirsty demons are entitled to their viewpoint as well!)

Lacking a clear logical basis for moral absolutism or a pragmatic basis for pure moral relativism, most real-world ethicists (politicians and diplomats) go for an ad hoc blend of the two in which frames, e.g. nations, remain essentially independent but are expected to agree on the "absolute goodness" of mutual tolerance. The idea is to find a goal that both frames have in common – survival, for instance – and encourage each frame to modify whatever ingredients might interfere with conflicting ingredients of the other frame to jeopardize the attainment of this common goal. Unfortunately, this strategy tends to fail where the main source of trouble is the irrational hostility of religious fundamentalists adhering literally to "holy writ" in which tolerance is literally banned (as it is banned by Islamic scripture, which literally calls for the subjugation or eradication of non-Islamic "infidels").

What, then, is the solution? That's a long story, so we'll merely outline it here. First, we need to mention several advanced concepts. One is utility; this means "value" and may vary by frame for any given thing. The greater the utility of something to a specific person or group, the higher its value. A utility function is a rule that assigns a personal or group value to something according to the values of its parameters. A rational utility function is one designed to maximize utility for those who apply it. Utilitarianism is a doctrine that prescribes "the greatest good for the greatest number" and provides us with a scale on which to measure an optimal solution involving multiple frames. And game (or decision) theory is a field of mathematics that tells players how to formulate winning, utility-maximizing strategies in various competitive scenarios or "games".

Game theory, which was initially formulated around the utility of individual players, was eventually found to give rise to paradoxes in which individual utility conflicts with the utility of one or more groups involved in the game. If enough players "cheat", i.e. defect from the group strategy in order to employ individual strategies that let them profit at the group's expense, the group infrastructure collapses, and where the wellbeing of the group is essential to that of its individual members, individual utility collapses as well. A player who cheats in such a game can thus end up cheating himself, coming away with far less than if he and others had played fair. Because a player's "rational" attempt to maximize his own personal gain can cause him to lose, the standard theory fails.

The extended version of game theory designed to resolve such paradoxes is called "the theory of metagames". Whereas standard game theory was designed to handle games analogous to chess and bridge, in which utility functions are assigned only to competing individuals, metagame theory is designed for games in which players belong to various groups, e.g. nations or religions, for which higher-level utility functions are also defined. In this case, utility is a combination of personal and group factors. Because the player's true utility function, which accounts for his group status, differs from that obtained when he considers only himself, the self is effectively "stratified". That is, a full definition of "self" must include all of the external relations tying the self to other selves at all levels of organization relevant to all possible games. This redefinition of "self" turns out to be of crucial importance across the entire ethical spectrum.

The theory of metagames permits the computation of strategic optima for any real-world scenario to which it can be properly applied (its proper application requires an accurate representation of the individual players and the groups to which they belong, the rules according to which they interact, and the overall context they share). This, of course, leads to a question: why has the theory not been used to solve all of the world's social problems? The reason: abstractly applying the theory is easier than concretely applying its results, especially in problematic situations where the ethical frames of the players are incompatible. Too often, circumstances that pit person against person, class against class and nation against nation also pit ethic against ethic and creed against creed. A lopsided ethic can encourage players to defect rather than accept the globally optimal solution, using stealth, subterfuge or superior force to achieve an inequitable outcome.

Because it leads to a stratification of self, the theory of metagames can be reduced to a single general self-based strategy: the Golden Rule. Because the Golden Rule distributes over all players in the global geopolitical metagame and is therefore absolute, those who defect from this strategy depart from absolute morality. In the case of the WTC tragedy, the reason for defection is clear: the Golden Rule is contradicted by the teachings of Islam, which isolates the self and utility functions of terrorists from those of their victims. This suggests that to successfully apply rational decision theory to the current situation, influential and well-meaning Moslems should appoint a council of Islamic scholars to revise Moslem scripture, excising specific passages that appear to mandate the slaughter of innocent people in the name of Islam. Only then can Moslems who prefer a literal, fundamentalist interpretation of holy writ earn a place in Paradise through prayer and good works rather than kamikaze terrorism.

Millennium Mouse: An Ecological Parable

There is a tiny cabin in the northern woods. Because it is tiny, it is easy to heat during the long, cold mountain winters. But because it is so warm and cozy, it is also a good winter abode for the mice that live in the surrounding hills. Each winter, a pair of mice finds a way into the cabin and makes a home there. If they were able to exercise good judgment, these mice would remain as unobtrusive as possible, taking a few stray crumbs and tidying up after themselves so as not to arouse the suspicion and ire of their hosts. Life would be warm and comfortable atop a ceiling beam over the potbelly stove, and enough crumbs would fall from the homeowners' plates to sustain their tiny guests. In fact, these little guests could even take pride in helping to keep the floors clean! They would live modestly until spring approached, have a single litter of pups, and then exit with their new family into the wide world outside the cabin as soon as the weather permitted. That way, when the coast was clear six or seven months later, those who had survived could use their old entranceway under the eaves and get cozy for another winter.

Unfortunately, this is simply not the nature of mice. First one pair comes in. Then another, and another. They begin to fight for territory, screaming at each other in the wee hours and sometimes even awakening their hosts. Soon, they are scrounging hungrily from table to stove to countertop, eliminating their bodily wastes even where the food that sustains them is prepared and served. Meanwhile, they breed copiously in nests made of materials torn from the private possessions of their hosts, wreaking havoc on bedding and furniture. Before long, the cabin undergoes a population explosion of filthy, destructive, combative little beasts that boldly rob their hosts right under their incredulous noses, urinating and defecating in the food supply to boot. And their hosts, being left with no choice, retaliate by setting a lethal gauntlet of spring traps, glue strips and poison bait. Mouse Armageddon ensues, and a pile of tiny bodies accumulates under the window.

In considering the self-destructive behavior of mice, human beings silently congratulate themselves on their superior judgment. "Mice are stupid to behave so injudiciously," they think. "If these mice just went easier on us, we might be able to tolerate them. But since they lack the intelligence to see this, we'll simply have to keep trapping and killing them." On the basis of such thoughts, one might almost think that human beings were innately wiser than mice with regard to such matters. But in this, one would be profoundly mistaken. For the only thing that separates the planet earth from that tiny cabin in the woods is size, and the cumulative effect of mankind on the earth is every bit as disgusting, from an ecological viewpoint, as that of mice on a cabin.

Being the evolutionary descendants of tiny mouselike proto-mammals, human beings are every bit as capable as mice of overpopulating, befouling and fighting over their living space, and there is no sane reason to think that the ultimate outcome will be any less unpleasant. After all, a mouse can always scurry from one cabin to another in an emergency. But when the earth is fouled beyond habitability, there will be no scurrying away from it, at least for the vast majority of us. Like mice, we will be trapped here and exterminated. And when that day comes, we will obviously not have our "superior intelligence" as a species to thank for it.

PART III

IQ, IEQ and Intelligence

In ordinary usage, the term *intelligence* is appreciably constrained by neither definition nor theory. Quite simply, there is no common agreement regarding what intelligence is or how it works. Accordingly, in the narrow context of psychometrics, the term denotes that which is measured by a narrow range of *IQ tests* exhibiting certain generic similarities, e.g., low-complexity items of stock varieties to be solved within strict time limits. In effect, psychometric standardization has led to a tautological and probably incorrect equation of IQ and intelligence that overrates the former and underrates the latter.

If a newly designed intelligence test differs from existing IQ tests in a way that could affect the precise identity or operant configuration of the measured attribute, then for reasons of logical consistency and descriptive clarity, it cannot be called an "IQ test". Though designed to measure intelligence, it will not necessarily perform this measurement in the same way that an IQ test performs it. Even if its preliminary data seem to correlate highly with IQ data, this is not proof that IQ is being directly measured; the test could be measuring some other set of mental performance factors which happens to coincide with IQ under more or less ambiguous conditions. Because resolving such issues can require more time and data than are readily available, it is inadvisable to call a test an "IQ test" if it differs markedly in structure or protocol from known members of the class.

To avoid the problem of rendering a specific *a priori* definition of what any such test will measure, it suffices to create a generic alternative description covering all tests which differ in structure or protocol from ordinary IQ tests, and for which high positive correlation with IQ has not yet been established.

This new term must refer to a measurable quantity that is specific to the tests it describes, and that may or may not equate to that which is measured by garden variety IQ tests. Since IQ is conventionally synonymous with "general intellectual ability", the term *IEQ* – standing for *Intellectual Efficacy* (or *Effect*) *Quantitator* – is the natural choice. IEQ denotes an arbitrary form of mental efficacy identical to performance on a specific test, thus circumventing questions regarding the extent to which that test measures exactly what is measured by ordinary IQ tests.

Although not every IEQ test is an IQ test, every IQ test is an IEQ test. IEQ is merely an effect-oriented generalization of IQ which spans certain quantifiable effects of that which we intuitively understand as "intelligence". Once it is established that a particular group of tests uniformly measures the same aspect of the same set of intelligence factors, the IEQ designation can be replaced with a more specific description ... e.g., the still-vague "IQ". But until then, the scientific need for clarity and consistency in the absence of a general theory of intelligence requires that IEQ replace IQ as the primary classification of any set of metrical constraints on intellectual production.

Far from being a semantical catchall, IEQ is rich in theoretical content. IEQ tests that are obviously measuring some aspect of what we understand as "intelligence", but display lower-than-normal positive correlation with ordinary IQ tests, are necessarily measuring a different kind or aspect of intelligence than is ordinarily measured. For example, consider those IEQ tests focussing on the extreme upper end of the intellectual scale, in which the mind lays protracted siege to very difficult problems of high intrinsic complexity. Here, where taking a test begins to resemble a persistent attack on a multifaceted, time-consuming real-world problem, computational demands placed on the mind may differ markedly from those associated with timed, low-complexity IQ tests. Extended concentration, multi-level parallelism, and intercontextual coordination of simultaneous subroutines begin to displace the sort of fire-and-forget linear computation involved in the completion of disconnected analogies, number series and picture sequences, and the spatial dimension of cognition starts to outweigh the temporal. Computational time and space become distinct "metafactors" of intelligence, respectively defining two possible directions – velocity and complexity – for the upward extrapolation of IQ. IEQ, spanning both directions, is the extrapolative medium.

There is an important additional reason for this change of terminology. While the benefits of professional standard- ization are often considerable, no scholarly or professional organization should be permitted to restrict scientific research, particularly in a field in desperate need of new ideas. Where this occurs, ideological politics can too easily lead to theoretical and methodological stagnation. In recent years, organized pressure has been successfully exerted on state legislatures to grant licensed psychologists exclusive proprietorship over the design, administration and scoring of IQ tests. In New York and California, for example, it is now illegal for a nonpsychologist to test intelligence or any other mental ability or attribute. While the intent is obviously to guard the public from psychological charlatanism while protecting the economic welfare of licensed psychologists, such laws do a tangible disservice not only to those talented amateurs with fresh ideas to contribute, but to the field as a whole.

Because the term IEQ denotes a measurement of *test-specific efficacy* rather than a general mental ability or attribute, it is not covered by the laws in question. The entirety of civilization is a product of the human intellect and thus a manifestation of intellectual efficacy; were only licensed psychologists permit- ted to measure intellectual efficacy, virtually no one but a licensed psychologist could measure anything not occurring in nature. For instance, because schoolwork is a manifestation of intellectual efficacy bearing a quantitative relationship to intellectual attributes like intelligence and imagination, no one but a licensed psychologist could legally grade schoolwork!

Once the conventional psychological distinction between mind and environment is suspended, there is no clear way to draw the line. Because language is the medium of law, jurisprudence amounts to an extended exercise in applied semantics. Consequently, no judge or jury can fail to recognize the clear and profound distinction between the near-antonyms ability, as resident in the mind, and effect or efficacy as expressed in the external environment ... especially when the science of psychology is explicitly defined on this very distinction.

A full account of the IQ-IEQ distinction would occupy many pages. However, two other points warrant quick mention. First, there is a subliminally potent near-homonymy between IQ and IEQ. Anyone who doubts it need merely say "IQ, IEQ" as rapidly as possible. And second, because statistical analysis is legally restricted only when applied to objects of legal restriction – and as we have just seen, IEQ is not such an object – IEQ tests can be tentatively normed with the use of whatever data might be deemed relevant. In other words, every raw score can be assigned an IEQ number bearing qualified description as an "IQ-extrapolated deviation", a percentile computed, and a "theoretical IQ equivalent" noted. Although every IEQ test should contain a disclaimer distinguishing the latter number from an IQ score – in some cases, converting it to an actual IQ would almost certainly require a substantial unknown correction factor – its inclusion is justified for orientative purposes.

For all of these reasons, amateur test designers and professional psychologists engaged in the construction, administration, or scoring of nonstandard "IQ tests" should immediately relabel their tests as suggested. In so doing, they can protect themselves from unjust legal prosecution, deflect ill-conceived proprietary resentment, and rest assured that they are helping to preserve the openness and integrity of much-needed research on the nature and application of human intelligence.

On High-Ceiling Intelligence Tests

Mensa, with a 1-in-50 qualification standard and hundreds of thousands of members worldwide, is the flagship of the high IQ community. Several years ago, the British barrister Lancelot Ware, one of the founders of Mensa, deplored the fact that it had strayed from its original purpose: to provide society with a pool of brilliant minds that could work on urgent problems too difficult for normal people to solve, including problems not falling within any single academic discipline. To his way of thinking, the proper function of high IQ societies like Mensa has always been to serve as an intellectual resource independent of academia. But as the years passed, it became evident to Ware and his fellow Founding Fathers that Mensa's primary function was not to solve pressing problems for the sake of all mankind, but to afford high-IQ people a chance to trade puzzles and socialize. Clearly disappointed, he likened Mensa's focus on puzzles and entertainment to "mental masturbation".

The super-high IQ community, consisting of a rising tower of societies with progressively more rarified qualification standards, is largely populated with Mensans and ex-Mensans who grew tired of their fun-loving compatriots in the HIQ melting pot. Yearning for higher standards of intellectual fellowship, they exhausted the ranges of ordinary IQ tests and designed new tests of their own, anchor-norming them on standard IQ test statistics in an attempt to extend their measurement capabilities. [To "anchor-norm" an intelligence test is to evaluate its statistics on the basis of known statistics on other tests taken by its subjects.] Since these tests must by definition consist of relatively harder problems – problems of greater intrinsic complexity than those found on ordinary IQ tests – they can take considerably more time to solve, often days or even weeks. On the other hand, the fact that ordinary IQ tests must be completed within a short period of time effectively limits the complexity of their items, thus limiting the degree to which they can measure one's ability to solve complex problems (i.e., one's "intelligence"). This limitation is referred to as the ceiling of the test.

Because not everyone has the time or money to sit for days or weeks in a psychologist's office working on a test, the new high-ceiling tests are typically untimed and unsupervised. In other words, they eliminate explicit constraints on speed and cheating. But careful consideration reveals that these constraints are either inappropriate or unnecessary for high-complexity tests. First, the speed factor of intellectual performance has been shown by such eminent psychologists as Arthur Jensen to be independent of "g", or pure fluid intelligence, and this means that the one who solves easy problems the most quickly need not be the one who can solve the hardest problems. For example, while Albert Einstein reputedly admitted to being a slow thinker, few would deny his extraordinary "intelligence", or ability to solve much harder problems than most people can solve. In addition, eliminating time constraints allows the subject to work on test problems when best able to focus, thus eliminating interference from factors like preoccupation and test anxiety. Second, cheating is possible only if test problems are already in circulation and their answers can be looked up or copied from the answer sheet of someone able to solve them. But if the problems are both new and so hard that those who can solve them are few and far between, then there is no book in which one can look up the test answers, and there is no nearby "A-student" from whose answer sheet one can copy. Every test subject is essentially on his or her own (of course, tests must be "retired" once verifiably correct answers begin circulating, e.g. via the Internet, but this takes considerably longer than might be expected).

One could no doubt find mainstream psychometricians who

disagree with the premise that intelligence can be accurately measured in this way. But just as there are said to be as many theories about any point of economics as there are economists, different psychometricians queried on the same point of intelligence and its measurement are apt to give different answers. Essentially, this owes to the fact that intelligence has never been satisfactorily defined; indeed, many would say that it has never been defined at all. The high-ceiling measurement strategy is as valid as any other in such a context, and more so for the following reason. Intuitively and historically, a genius is somebody who can recognize and formulate an important problem and then solve it, even if it takes years to do so. He (or she) who succeeds in locating and solving even a single great problem earns the title. High-ceiling tests are merely an attempt to take intelligence testing in this direction, replacing the speedy solution of shallow problems with the thoughtful, methodical solution of deeper problems. Because the value of ordinary IQ tests resides entirely in the accuracy with which they predict the ability to solve deep problems outside the examination room, and thus in the prediction of real-world intellectual achievement, high-ceiling tests are in some ways superior to their timed counterparts; they afford direct access to something that ordinary IQ tests can measure only indirectly. In this light, it almost appears that the statistical dependencies should be reversed, and that ordinary IQ tests should be anchor-normed on high-ceiling test statistics.

The issues outlined above tie into another crucial psychometric distinction, that between ratio IQ and deviation IQ. Originally, IQ literally meant "intelligence quotient"; it was defined as the ratio of mental age to chronological age, multiplied by 100. Thus, an intellectually precocious child who exhibits the same problem-solving ability as a normal older child has a "high (ratio) IQ". Unfortunately, the number of extremely high ratio scores varies with age; most of the highest scores are generated by young children, making it falsely appear that the incidence of genius decreases as children approach adulthood. This has precipitated a shift of emphasis to deviation IQ, which ranks a subject's raw test score within the subject's own chronological age group (it is called "deviation IQ" because it is gauged in terms of a common if somewhat oxymoronic statistical measure, the standard deviation). By "grading on the curve" with respect to age, psychometrics avoids the absurd conclusion that genius is mainly a prerogative of childhood.

The distinctions among chronological age groups reflect distinctions in precisely what is being measured within each group. Simplistically, we can reduce these distinctions to a single distinction between two related but inequivalent criteria, relative acceleration of mental development during childhood and relative level of mental development finally achieved. This implies that developmental precocity cannot be regarded as an infallible predictor of adult mental development; there is no guarantee that a child's IQ, as expressed in terms of deviation from the mean within his or her chronological age group, will turn out to be an accurate measure of terminal problem-solving ability. In principle, it is possible for children whose minds develop at different rates to finally achieve the same level of adult problem-solving ability, and for children in a developmental dead heat to finally achieve different levels of adult problem-solving ability. Since it is adult problem-solving ability that is important – after all, it is adults who are responsible for solving society's important problems – childhood (developmental) IQ ultimately takes a back seat to adult IQ. And because genius-level adult IQ can only be measured by high-ceiling, high-complexity power tests of the kind described above, it makes sense to use power tests as primary qualification instruments for super-HIQ "genius societies".

But even though childhood IQ and adult IQ are not perfectly synonymous, there is enough of a connection between them to justify the treatment of extremely precocious children as a precious human resource. This is why many in the super-

HIQ community have become interested in establishing a "mentoring program" in which identifiably gifted children can receive advice and encouragement from high-intelligence adults. By combining such projects with sincere attempts to solve a few of the more urgent problems facing humanity (and the accompanying material deals with one such attempt), perhaps the high-IQ community can salvage Lance Ware's idealistic dream after all.

The counselors and psychologists of the world's public education systems have a practical problem, namely how to determine which students should receive what kinds of attention. Due to the practical constraints within which this problem must be solved, certain convenient psychometric assumptions have been adopted, and as is often the case with such assumptions, claims of factuality and absolutism eventually follow. Before long, exceptions are ruled out on what amounts to an *a priori* basis. But reality refuses to be confined by the strictures of dogma, and bad assumptions eventually unravel despite their convenience. Human intelligence is almost certainly a case in point; once a person emerges from the artificial world of formal education, there are other, more accurate ways to gauge intelligence ... other protocols. Ultimately, the only measure of genius is intellectual production, and if standard IQ tests fail to predict its presence or absence in any given case, then it is they (and not the productions) that must be considered "invalid".

Before closing, I should mention that it is my personal belief that although IQ tests can at times afford insight into human intelligence, intelligence is far too protean to be definitively determined by IQ tests (particularly the rigid tests and testing protocols of mainstream psychometrics, which presume that intelligence can always be pinned down and accurately measured at the one-sided convenience of educators and psychologists). There is far more to it than that. The mind of every human being is a microcosm, and the only real issue is his or her access to the associated intellectual potential at a given point in time, with respect to a given set of tasks. While those consistently displaying relatively high levels of access to their potential may be better-equipped to shine in contexts that put a high premium on abstract thought, the sheer complexity of human psychology precludes the absolute measurement of human intelligence by currently available means. Perhaps in the future, it will be possible to scan a person's brain and infer limitations on its capabilities from elements of structure and neural reflex alone. But that time has not yet come.

On Absolute Truth and Knowledge

First, a word on the title of this essay. *Absolute knowledge* is absolutely true, and *absolute truth* is the definitive predicate of absolute knowledge. That is, if something is known with absolute certainty, then it can be subjected to tests affirming its truth, while if something can be affirmatively tested for truth, then it is known with certainty by the tester. This applies whether the tests in question are perceptual or inferential. Where knowledge can denote either direct embodiment or internal modeling by an arbitrary system, and *test* denotes a straightforward systemic efficacy criterion, *knower* and *tester* can refer to reality at large. In this generalization, truth and knowledge are identical. While it is possible to split, splice and braid countless philosophical hairs over the connotations respectively attached to truth and knowledge, this simple generalized relationship conveniently spares us the necessity. It is with this express understanding that these terms and phrases are employed herein.

To perceive one and the same reality, human beings need a kind of "absolute knowledge" wired into their minds and nervous systems. The structure and physiology of their brains, nerves and sense organs provide them, at least in part, with elementary cognitive and perceptual categories and relationships in terms of which to apprehend the world. This "absolute" kind of knowledge is what compels the perceptions and logical inferences of any number of percipients to be mutually consistent, and to remain consistent over time and space. Without the *absoluteness* of such knowledge – without its universality and invariance – we could not share a common reality; our minds and senses would lie and bicker without respite, precipitating us into mental and sensory chaos. Time

THE ART OF KNOWING

and space, mind and matter, would melt back into the haze of undifferentiated potential from which the universe is born.

Given the fact that absolute knowledge is a requisite of our collective ability to sustain a perceptually consistent universe, it is nothing short of astonishing that there are people who react with incredulity or derision at any mention of its possible existence. Their attitude seems to be that the very idea smacks of "hubris", being nothing but an empty pretense exceeding the capacity of the small and overly-challenged human mind. The truth, however, is that hubris is nowhere more evident than among those holding irrational opinions in contempt of logic, and denying the existence of absolute knowledge is a case in point. In fact, the entire history of philosophy and science can be characterized as an undying quest for absolute knowledge ... a timeless attempt to comprehensively extend the *a priori* and analytical into the realm of the apparently *a posteriori* and synthetic. This quest includes the efforts of researchers from many fields, from physics and cosmology to philosophy and computer science.

The Holy Grail of this quest is known as the TOE, or *Theory of Everything*. A TOE purports to be absolute truth by an implicit *reductio ad absurdum*: if it does not constitute absolute truth, then its truth can be relativized to a partial context within reality at large, in which case it is not a theory of *everything*. Thus, if a TOE exists, it falls squarely under the heading of absolute knowledge. But unfortunately, the proper method for constructing such a theory has not been entirely obvious, particularly to theorists steeped in the ambiguities and paradoxes of four centuries of post-Cartesian science and philosophy. As science has advanced and philosophy has wearily tried to keep pace, their once-stentorian claims of absolute truth have been all but extinguished, and the mainstream search for a TOE has lately been pursued without a clear understanding of what is being sought.

The apparent absence of a TOE notwithstanding, has any kind of absolute knowledge ever been scientifically formulated?

Yes, in the form of *logical tautologies*. A tautology is a sentential relation, i.e. a formula consisting of variables and logical connectives, with the property that it is true for all possible assignments of Boolean truth values (*true* or *false*) to its variables. For example, the statement "if *x* is a sentence, then either *x* or *not-x* (but not both) must be true" is a tautology because no matter which truth values are consistently applied to *x* and *not-x*, the statement is unequivocally true. Indeed, tautologies comprise the axioms and theorems of 2-valued logic itself, and because all meaningful theories necessarily conform to 2-valued logic, define the truth concept for all of the sciences. From mathematics and physics to biology and psychology, logical tautologies reign supreme and inviolable.

That a tautology constitutes absolute truth can be proven as follows. First, logic is absolute within any system for which (a) the complementary truth values T (true) and F (false) correspond to systemic inclusion and exclusion, a semantic necessity without which meaningful reference is impossible; and (b) lesser predicates and their complements equal subsystemic inclusion and exclusion. Because a tautology is an axiom of 2-valued logic, violating it disrupts the T/F distinction and results in the corruption of informational boundaries between perceptual and cognitive predicates recognized or applied in the system, as well as between each predicate and its negation. Thus, the observable fact that perceptual boundaries are intact across reality at large implies that no tautology within its *syntax*, or set of structural and functional rules, has been violated; indeed, if such a tautology ever *were* violated, then reality would disintegrate due to corruption of the informational boundaries which define it. So a tautology is "absolute truth" not only with respect to logic, but with respect to reality at large.

What does this mean? Uncertainty or non-absoluteness of truth value always involves some kind of confusion or ambiguity regarding the distinction between the sentential predicates *true* and *false*. Where these predicates are applied to a more specific predicate and its negation – e.g., "it is *true* that the earth is round and *false* that the earth is not-round" – the confusion devolves to the contextual distinction between these lesser predicates, in this case *round* and *not-round* within the context of *the earth*. Because all of the ambiguity can be localized to a specific distinction in a particular context, it presents no general problem for reality at large; we can be uncertain about whether or not the earth is round without disrupting the logic of reality in general. However, where a statement is directly about reality in general, any disruption of or ambiguity regarding the T/F distinction disrupts the distinction between *reality* and *not-reality*. Were such a disruption to occur at the level of basic cognition or perception, reality would become impossible to perceive, recognize, or acknowledge as something that "exists".

By definition, this is the case with regard to our cognitive-perceptual *syntax*, the set of structural and inferential rules governing perception and cognition in general. Since a tautology is a necessary and universal element of this syntax, tautologies can under no circumstances be violated within reality. Thus, they are "absolute knowledge". We may not be able to specify every element of absolute knowledge, but we can be sure of two things about it: that it *exists* in reality to the full extent necessary to guarantee its non-violation, and that no part of it yet to be determined can violate absolute knowledge already in hand. Whether or not we can write up an exhaustive itemized list of absolute truths, we can be sure that such a list exists, and that its contents are sufficiently "recognizable" by reality at large to ensure their functionality. Absolute truth, being essential to the integrity of reality, *must exist* on the level of reference associated with the preservation of global consistency, and may thus be duly incorporated in a theory of reality.

On the other hand, the fact that any reasonable definition of "absolute truth" amounts to tautology can be shown by reversing this reasoning. Since absolute truth must be *universal*, it is always true regardless of the truth values of its variables (where the variables actually represent objects and systems for which specific state-descriptions vary in space and time with respect to truth value). Moreover, it falls within its own scope and is thus *self-referential*. By virtue of its universality and self-reference, it is a universal element of *reality syntax*, the set of structural and functional rules governing the spatial structure and temporal evolution of reality. As such, it must be *unfalsifiable*, any supposition of its falsehood leading directly to a *reductio ad absurdum*. And to ice the cake, it is unavoidably implicated in its own justification; were it ever to be violated, the T/F boundary would be disrupted, and this would prevent it (or anything else) from being proven. Therefore, it is an active constraint in its own proof, and thus possesses all the characteristics of a tautology.

To recap, the characteristic attributes of a logical tautology are as follows: (1) it cannot be disobeyed, which implies that it has universal scope and thus accepts and truthfully predicates all closed sentential (predicative) structures, including itself *and logic in its entirety*, under assignment to its own variables; and (2) it is self-affirming or self-justifying and figures in its own definition or demonstration within the associated grammar. Obviously, (1) and (2) are not independent; (1) implies that a tautology is a universal, self-similar, metalogical *element of syntax* of the language and metalanguages of which it is a part, while (2) says that it is a *critical* element of syntax that cannot be eliminated without compromising the integrity of the syntax as a whole (thus, any supposition that it is false or eliminable reduces itself to absurdity by syntactic rules of inference, forcing the syntax to "protect itself" through *reductio ad absurdum*). Since any reasonable syntactic and/or semantic definition of *absolute truth* bestows upon it the properties of necessity and truthwise invariance with respect to content, it is unquestionably tautological in nature.

Accordingly, it is desirable to formulate reality theory as a tautology. To whatever extent this can be done, the theory constitutes "absolute knowledge" and is therefore eligible as a TOE. This suffices to show that if the form of absolute knowledge hopefully referred to as a TOE exists, it must be tautological. Next we will show that a TOE and its universe can be related in such a way that the theory is semantically tautological *with respect to its universe*, i.e. that (a) the theory is intrinsically tautological, and (b) its tautological structure is modeled by its universe. And in the course of doing so, we will show that it is indeed possible to ensure by the method of constructing this theory that its universe coincides with reality at large, and thus that it constitutes a valid theory of reality. Specifically, the construction will incorporate one or more attributes that are necessarily modeled by reality at large, and that simultaneously ensure the theory's tautological structure.

How can a TOE, or comprehensive theory of reality, be structured as a tautology? First, by definition, a TOE is *universal*; this is implied by the E, which stands for *Everything*. Thus, it is comprehensive. Second, it is *self-referential*; a theory of everything, being a part of the "everything" to which it refers, must refer to itself. More precisely, a TOE must be totally recursive in a manner analogous to logic, each atom referring exclusively to other parts of the theory, and be able to refer to itself *in part and in whole* in order to possess full logical closure. This can be arranged by incorporating one or more self-representative variables and their definitive relationships, up to and including a dynamic variable representing the theory as a whole (in fact, the theory can incorporate a "hology" predicate that goes considerably farther; instead of merely containing itself as a variable, a theory equipped with such a predicate can *everywhere* contain itself by virtue of self–similarity or self–distribution). Because it represents a theory of perceptual reality, this variable contains all elements of cognitive syntax and their perceptual contents; since variables can be defined in general terms without specifically enumerating their contents, we do not need to know exactly what it contains in order to use it. And third, because logic is the primary ingredient of cognitive-perceptual syntax, the self-referential TOE refers to logic in part and in whole and is therefore *metalogical*. Thus, it can incorporate a kind of ultimate truth predicate that asserts its own tautological structure and guarantees that no matter what (semantic and other) kinds of paradox may *arise* within the theory, they can always be *resolved* within the theory. A theory possessing all three of these properties is called a *supertautology*, denoting the reality-theoretic counterpart of a logical tautology.

Let us now attend to some of the details of constructing a supertautology. First, we repose the *a priori* and analytic knowledge that we are given in the form of cognitive syntax, including logic and all of its implications, in a variable to which we apply (a) the rules of logic itself; (b) three recursively-related metalogical axioms that are themselves true *a priori* and analytically implied by each other (in a word, *self-evident*). Note again that in creating and assigning content to this variable, we do not have to enumerate all of its contents; we can refer to them *en masse* by their joint characteristic, namely the "absoluteness" necessary to ensure perceptual and inferential consistency. Since a theory falls under the mathematical definition of a *language*, it is natural to refer to the contents in question as the "rules of syntax" of that language, or simply as its *syntax*; thus, the TOE recursively contains a variable representing its own syntax, permitting the manipulation of that variable and the grammatical extraction of its implications according to syntactic rules. This recursive construction makes the "absoluteness" of the variable (and theory) *logically heritable*, conferring absoluteness on whatever is inferred within the system. Together, the "implicate" variable and its "explicate" theoretic medium comprise a bootstrapped extension of the self-referential syntax of logic itself, letting that syntax be "mined" for a potential wealth of hidden analytic content.

The key to applying this knowledge scientifically is the

semantic functionality of the three metalogical axioms adjoining the object-level syntax. Conveniently, these (recursively related) axioms can be thought of in terms of a trio of property-principle pairs, the "Three Cs" and the "Three Ms". The Cs are three properties that a TOE must inevitably possess, namely *Comprehensiveness*, *Closure* and *Consistency*, while the Ms are metalogical axioms respectively associated with those properties. These principles are the *Mind Equals Reality Principle* (associated with comprehensiveness), the *Metaphysical Autology Principle* (associated with closure), and the *Multiplex Unity Principle* (associated with consistency), respectively abbreviated M=R, MAP and MU. We have already been partially introduced to these principles in all but name, and in any case need only one of them to proceed farther: M=R. Concisely, M=R asserts that there exists a semantic (language-to-universe) correspondence between objective reality and the absolute subjective rules of perception and inference, i.e. cognitive and perceptual syntax. This correspondence defines a morphism, *incoversion*, predicating the assignment of a certain structural predicate, *hology*, to the universe-language / metalanguage system (see Introduction to the CTMU).

Hology, a special kind of self-similarity conferring super-tautological status, equals the relationship of the TOE and its universe to the self-representative variable by which it is encapsulated. Hology means that the syntax by which reality configures, recognizes and processes itself is the image of a distributed endomorphism, the incoversion morphism, surjecting the objective *self-intersect* (distributed component) of reality onto every interior point and region of reality as transductive syntactic potential, i.e. as general rules of transduction to be variously expressed by objects at any location. Although real objects generally access and express only a small part of this syntax, combinations of interacting objects may express and access more of it by mutual input-to-output behavioral transduction; through this kind of behavioral transduction, the self-intersect, though generally composed of distributed rules applying everywhere in reality, resolves to a *Distributed Conditional Form* (DCF) explicitly containing all of the local systems and states generated by those rules. The self-intersect and its DCF resolution comprise the syntax and language of reality. Because hology maps the *reality* syntax to our *cognitive* syntax – because the self-intersect plays dual objective and subjective roles – perceptible objects and processes tautologically conform to our innate perceptual categories, making the TOE a *supertautology* comprising the purest and most universal kind of absolute truth.

The above reasoning subjects the absolute (*a priori*) knowledge in our minds to a kind of recursive "squaring" operation, causing it to self-explicate as its own medium and projecting it onto external reality. This repetitive operation resembles the mutual reflection of a pair of polymorphic mirrors, one labeled *mind* and the other labeled *reality*, that faithfully reflect each other's evolving image. Although one might suspect that the tautological nature of the construction renders it barren of interest, this would be akin to saying that a squaring operation never yields more than the original number. While that might be true for a featureless numeric identity (e.g. $1^2 = 1$), the cognitive syntax of the human mind is far from "featureless". In recursive self-combination, it is capable of generating a universe, and a theory constructed according to this recursive relationship is capable of veridically *capturing* that universe. Indeed, there is a sense in which the TOE, and all of the absolute knowledge it holds, is *identical to the universe it describes*. But the meaning of this statement – and it is a statement that is pregnant with meaning – lies beyond the purpose at hand.

The CTMU is a theory of reality, or TOE, that has been constructed according to this blueprint. If, as a rationalist, one insists that absolute truth and knowledge are exclusively mathematical, then the CTMU is mathematics; if, as an empiricist, one insists that they reside exclusively in our direct perceptions of reality, then the CTMU is embodied in our direct perceptions of reality (including our direct perceptions of the *comprehensiveness, closure* and *consistency* of reality). The truth, of course, is that by the method of its construction, it is both. But in any case, would-be pundits who cling blindly to folk-epistemological "absolutes" like *truth is never more than provisional, science is inherently without stability and there are no such things as absolute truth and knowledge* are urgently in need of an intellectual awakening, and until it comes, should refrain from disseminating their irrational opinions to others who might gullibly mistake them for fact. Such truisms have their contexts, but these contexts do not include the highest levels of discourse regarding truth and knowledge, and they do not include the CTMU.

There is, of course, more to the CTMU than just its supertautological structure. For example, it incorporates a new conceptualization of spacetime, resolves numerous high level reality-theoretic paradoxes, and establishes a bridge between science and theology, all with considerably more detail than this brief monograph allows. But as regards "absolute truth and knowledge", its status as a supertautology is necessary and sufficient to explain why it is uniquely qualified for the title. If the simplicity and elegance of its design seems "too obvious", "too convenient" or "too good to be true", this is certainly no fault of the theory or its author; at best, it testifies to the opacity of certain formerly useful but outworn conceptual barriers erected in science and philosophy over the last several centuries, and to the inertia of the scientific and academic establishments which tend them.

One final note. The CTMU is neither intended nor presented as an encyclopedic compendium of absolute truth. It is meant only to provide a comprehensive, consistent and self-contained (and to that extent "absolute") logical framework for bridging the gaps between apparently unrelated fields of knowledge, helping to locate and correct fundamental inconsistencies within and among these fields, and developing new kinds of knowledge that might arise from the intersections of fields which already exist. Because the real universe is everywhere in the process of self-creation, human knowledge can and must continue to grow. The CTMU is intended not as a brittle, undersized pot that will root-bind and choke this growing knowledge, but as fertile and well-aerated soil through which it can spread. By its very design, the CTMU will continue to accommodate and accelerate our intellectual progress ... and since there is no other theory that fully *shares* its design, it is irreplaceable for that purpose.

This completes our introduction to the topic of absolute truth and knowledge.

The Theory of Theories

You know what they say about theories: *everybody's got one.* In fact, some people have a theory about pretty much every-thing. That's not one Master Theory of Everything, mind you ... that's a separate theory about every little thing under the sun. (To have a Master Theory, you have to be able to tie all those little theories together.)

But what is a "theory"? Is a theory just a story that you can make up about something, being as fanciful as you like? Or does a theory at least have to seem like it might be true? Even more stringently, is a theory something that has to be rendered in terms of logical and mathematical symbols, and described in plain language only after the original chicken-scratches have made the rounds in academia?

A theory is all of these things. A theory can be good or bad, fanciful or plausible, true or false. The only firm requirements are that it (1) have a subject, and (2) be stated in a language in terms of which the subject can be coherently described. Where these criteria hold, the theory can always be "formalized", or translated into the symbolic language of logic and mathematics. Once formalized, the theory can be subjected to various mathematical tests for truth and internal consistency.

But doesn't that essentially make "theory" synonymous with "description"? Yes. A theory is just a description of something. If we can use the logical implications of this description to relate the components of that something to other components in revealing ways, then the theory is said to have "explanatory power". And if we can use the logical implications of the description to make correct predictions about how that something behaves under various conditions,

121

then the theory is said to have "predictive power".

From a practical standpoint, in what kinds of theories should we be interested? Most people would agree that in order to be interesting, a theory should be about an important subject ... a subject involving something of use or value to us, if even on a purely abstract level. And most would also agree that in order to help us extract or maximize that value, the theory must have explanatory or predictive power. For now, let us call any theory meeting both of these criteria a "serious" theory.

Those interested in serious theories include just about everyone, from engineers and stockbrokers to doctors, automobile mechanics and police detectives. Practically anyone who gives advice, solves problems or builds things that function needs a serious theory from which to work. But three groups who are especially interested in serious theories are scientists, mathematicians and philosophers. These are the groups which place the strictest requirements on the theories they use and construct.

While there are important similarities among the kinds of theories dealt with by scientists, mathematicians and philosophers, there are important differences as well. The most important differences involve the subject matter of the theories. Scientists like to base their theories on experiment and observation of the real world ... not on perceptions themselves, but on what they regard as concrete "objects of the senses". That is, they like their theories to be *empirical*. Mathematicians, on the other hand, like their theories to be essentially *rational* ... to be based on logical inference regarding abstract mathematical objects existing in the mind, independently of the senses. And philosophers like to pursue broad theories of reality aimed at relating these two kinds of object. (This actually mandates a third kind of object, the *infocognitive syntactic operator* ... but another time.)

Of the three kinds of theory, by far the lion's share of popular reportage is commanded by theories of science. Unfortunately, this presents a problem. For while science owes a huge debt to philosophy and mathematics – it can be characterized as the child of the former and the sibling of the latter – it does not even treat them as its equals. It treats its parent, philosophy, as unworthy of consideration. And although it tolerates and uses mathematics at its convenience, relying on mathematical reasoning at almost every turn, it acknowledges the remarkable obedience of objective reality to mathematical principles as little more than a cosmic "lucky break".

Science is able to enjoy its meretricious relationship with mathematics precisely because of its queenly dismissal of philosophy. By refusing to consider the philosophical relationship between the abstract and the concrete on the supposed grounds that philosophy is inherently impractical and unproductive, it reserves the right to ignore that relationship even while exploiting it in the construction of scientific theories. And exploit the relationship it certainly does! There is a scientific platitude stating that if one cannot put a number to one's data, then one can prove nothing at all. But insofar as numbers are arithmetically and algebraically related by various mathematical structures, the platitude amounts to a thinly veiled affirmation of the mathematical basis of knowledge.

Although scientists like to think that everything is open to scientific investigation, they have a rule that explicitly allows them to screen out certain facts. This rule is called the *scientific method*. Essentially, the scientific method says that every scientist's job is to:

1. Observe something in the world.
2. Invent a theory to fit the observations.
3. Use the theory to make predictions.
4. Experimentally or observationally test the predictions.
5. Modify the theory in light of any new findings.
6. Repeat the cycle from step 3 onward.

In fact, if we regard the scientific method as a theory about the nature and acquisition of scientific knowledge (and we can), it is not a theory of knowledge in general. It is only a theory of things accessible to the senses. Worse yet, it is a theory only of sensible things that have two further attributes: they are non-universal and can therefore be distinguished from the rest of sensory reality, and they can be seen by multiple observers who are able to "replicate" each other's observations under like conditions. Needless to say, there is no reason to assume that these attributes are necessary even in the sensory realm. The first describes nothing general enough to coincide with reality as a whole – for example, the homogeneous medium of which reality consists, or an abstract mathematical principle that is everywhere true – and the second describes nothing that is either subjective, like human consciousness, or objective but rare and unpredictable ... e.g. ghosts, UFOs and yetis, of which jokes are made but which may, given the number of individual witnesses reporting them, correspond to real phenomena.

The fact that the scientific method does not permit the investigation of abstract mathematical principles is especially embarrassing in light of one of its more crucial steps: "invent a theory to fit the observations." A theory happens to be a logical and/or mathematical construct whose basic elements of description are mathematical units and relationships. If the scientific method were interpreted as a blanket description of reality, which is all too often the case, the result would go something like this: "Reality consists of all and only that to which we can apply a protocol which cannot be applied to its own (mathematical) ingredients and is therefore unreal." Mandating the use of "unreality" to describe "reality" is rather questionable in anyone's protocol.

What about mathematics itself? The fact is, science is not the only walled city in the intellectual landscape. With equal and opposite prejudice, the mutually exclusionary methods of mathematics and science guarantee their continued separation despite the (erstwhile) best efforts of philosophy. While science hides behind the scientific method, which effectively excludes from investigation its own mathematical ingredients, mathematics divides itself into "pure" and "applied" branches and explicitly divorces the "pure" branch from the real world. Notice that this makes "applied" synonymous with "impure". Although the field of applied mathematics by definition contains every practical use to which mathematics has ever been put, it is viewed as "not quite mathematics" and therefore beneath the consideration of any "pure" mathematician.

In place of the scientific method, pure mathematics relies on a principle called the *axiomatic method*. The axiomatic method begins with a small number of self-evident statements called *axioms* and a few *rules of inference* through which new statements, called *theorems*, can be derived from existing statements. In a way parallel to the scientific method, the axiomatic method says that every mathematician's job is to:

1. Conceptualize a class of mathematical objects.

2. Isolate its basic elements, its most general and self-evident principles, and the rules by which its truths can be derived from those principles.

3. Use those principles and rules to derive theorems, define new objects, and formulate new propositions about the extended set of theorems and objects.

4. Prove or disprove those propositions.

5. Where the proposition is true, make it a theorem and add it to the theory.

6. Repeat from step 3 onwards.

The scientific and axiomatic methods are like mirror images of each other, but located in opposite domains. Just replace "observe" with "conceptualize" and "part of the world" with "class of mathematical objects", and the analogy practically completes itself. Little wonder, then, that scientists and mathematicians often profess mutual respect. However, this conceals an imbalance. For while the activity of the mathematician is integral to the scientific method, that of the scientist is irrelevant to mathematics (except for the kind of scientist called a "computer scientist", who plays the role of ambassador between the two realms). At least in principle, the mathematician is more necessary to science than the scientist is to mathematics.

As a philosopher might put it, the scientist and the mathematician work on opposite sides of the Cartesian divider between mental and physical reality. If the scientist stays on his own side of the divider and merely accepts what the mathematician chooses to throw across, the mathematician does just fine. On the other hand, if the mathematician does not throw across what the scientist needs, then the scientist is in trouble. Without the mathematician's functions and equations from which to build scientific theories, the scientist would be confined to little more than taxonomy. As far as making quantitative predictions were concerned, he or she might as well be guessing the number of jellybeans in a candy jar.

From this, one might be tempted to theorize that the axiomatic method does not suffer from the same kind of inadequacy as does the scientific method ... that it, and it alone, is sufficient to discover all of the abstract truths rightfully claimed as "mathematical". But alas, that would be too convenient. In 1931, an Austrian mathematical logician named Kurt Gödel proved that there are true mathematical statements that cannot be proven by means of the axiomatic method. Such statements are called "undecidable". Gödel's finding rocked the intellectual world to such an extent that even today, mathematicians, scientists and philosophers alike are struggling to figure out how best to weave the loose thread of undecidability into the seamless fabric of reality.

To demonstrate the existence of undecidability, Gödel used a simple trick called *self-reference*. Consider the statement "this sentence is false." It is easy to dress this statement up as a logical formula. Aside from being true or false, what else could such a formula say about itself? Could it pronounce itself, say, unprovable? Let's try it: "This formula is unprovable". If the given formula is in fact unprovable, then it is true and therefore a theorem. Unfortunately, the axiomatic method cannot recognize it as such without a proof. On the other hand, suppose it is provable. Then it is self-apparently false (because its provability belies what it says of itself) and yet true (because provable without respect to content)! It seems that we still have the makings of a paradox ... a statement that is "unprovably provable" and therefore absurd.

But what if we now introduce a distinction between *levels* of proof? For example, what if we define a *metalanguage* as a language used to talk about, analyze or prove things regarding statements in a lower-level *object language*, and call the base level of Gödel's formula the "object" level and the higher (proof) level the "metalanguage" level? Now we have one of two things: a statement that can be metalinguistically *proven* to be linguistically *unprovable*, and thus recognized as a theorem conveying valuable information about the limitations of the object language, or a statement that cannot be metalinguistically proven to be linguistically unprovable, which, though uninformative, is at least no paradox. Voilà: self-reference without paradox! It turns out that "this formula is unprovable" can be translated into a generic example of an undecidable mathematical truth. Because the associated reasoning involves a metalanguage of mathematics, it is called "metamathematical".

It would be bad enough if undecidability were the only thing inaccessible to the scientific and axiomatic methods together. But the problem does not end there. As we noted above, mathematical truth is only one of the things that the scientific method cannot touch. The others include not only rare and unpredictable phenomena that cannot be easily captured by microscopes, telescopes and other scientific instruments, but things that are too large or too small to be captured, like the whole universe and the tiniest of subatomic particles; things that are "too universal" and therefore indiscernable, like the homogeneous medium of which reality consists; and things that are "too subjective", like human consciousness, human emotions, and so-called "pure qualities" or *qualia*. Because mathematics has thus far offered no means of compensating for these scientific blind spots, they continue to mark holes in our picture of scientific and mathematical reality.

But mathematics has its own problems. Whereas science suffers from the problems just described – those of indiscernability and induction, nonreplicability and subjectivity – mathematics suffers from undecidability. It therefore seems natural to ask whether there might be any other inherent weaknesses in the combined methodology of math and science. There are indeed. Known as the *Löwenheim–Skolem theorem* and the *Duhem–Quine thesis*, they are the respective stock-in-trade of disciplines called *model theory* and the *philosophy of science* (like any parent, philosophy always gets the last word). These weaknesses have to do with ambiguity ... with the difficulty of telling whether a given theory applies to one thing or another, or whether one theory is "truer" than another with respect to what both theories purport to describe.

But before giving an account of Löwenheim–Skolem and Duhem–Quine, we need a brief introduction to model theory. Model theory is part of the logic of "formalized theories", a branch of mathematics dealing rather self-referentially with the structure and interpretation of theories that have been couched in the symbolic notation of mathematical logic ... that is, in the kind of mind-numbing chicken-scratches that everyone but a mathematician loves to hate. Since any worthwhile theory can be formalized, model theory is a *sine qua non* of meaningful theorization.

Let's make this short and punchy. We start with *propositional logic*, which consists of nothing but tautological, always-true relationships among sentences represented by single variables. Then we move to *predicate logic*, which considers the content of these sentential variables ... what the sentences actually say. In general, these sentences use symbols called *quantifiers* to assign attributes to variables semantically representing mathematical or real-world objects. Such assignments are called "predicates". Next, we consider *theories*, which are complex predicates that break down into systems of related predicates; the *universes* of theories, which are the mathematical or real-world systems described by the theories; and the descriptive correspondences themselves, which are called *interpretations*. A *model* of a theory is any interpretation under which all of the theory's statements are true. If we refer to a theory as an *object language* and to its referent as an *object universe*, the intervening model can only be described and validated in a metalanguage of the language-universe complex.

Though formulated in the mathematical and scientific realms respectively, Löwenheim–Skolem and Duhem–Quine can be thought of as opposite sides of the same model-theoretic coin. Löwenheim–Skolem says that a theory cannot in general distinguish between two different models; for example, any true theory about the numeric relationship of points on a continuous line segment can also be interpreted as a theory of the integers (counting numbers). On the other hand, Duhem–Quine says that two theories cannot in general be distinguished on the basis of any observation statement regarding the universe.

Just to get a rudimentary feel for the subject, let's take a closer look at the Duhem–Quine thesis. *Observation statements*, the raw data of science, are statements that can be proven true or false by observation or experiment. But observation is not independent of theory; an observation is always interpreted in some theoretical context. So an experiment in physics is not merely an observation, but the *interpretation* of an observation. This leads to the *Duhem Thesis*, which states that scientific observations and experiments cannot invalidate isolated hypotheses, but only whole sets of theoretical statements at once. This is because a theory T composed of various laws $\{L_i\}$, $i = 1, 2, 3, \ldots$ almost never entails an observation statement except in conjunction with various auxiliary hypotheses $\{A_j\}$, $j = 1, 2, 3, \ldots$. Thus, an observation statement at most disproves the complex $\{L_i + A_j\}$.

To take a well-known historical example, let $T = \{L_1, L_2, L_3\}$ be Newton's three laws of motion, and suppose that these laws seem to entail the observable consequence that the orbit of the planet Uranus is O. But in fact, Newton's laws alone do not determine the orbit of Uranus. We must also consider things like the presence or absence of other forces, other nearby bodies that might exert appreciable gravitational influence on Uranus, and so on. Accordingly, determining the orbit of Uranus requires auxiliary hypotheses like $A_1 =$ "only gravitational forces act on the planets", $A_2 =$ "the total number of solar planets, including Uranus, is 7," et cetera. So if the orbit in question is found to differ from the predicted value O, then instead of simply invalidating the theory T of Newtonian mechanics, this observation invalidates the entire complex of laws and auxiliary hypotheses $T = \{L_1, L_2, L_3; A_1, A_2, \ldots\}$. It would follow that at least one element of this complex is false, but which one? Is there any 100% sure way to decide?

As it turned out, the weak link in this example was the hypothesis $A_2 =$ "the total number of solar planets, including Uranus, is 7". In fact, there turned out to be an additional large planet, Neptune, which was subsequently sought and located precisely because this hypothesis (A_2) seemed open to doubt. But unfortunately, there is no general rule for making such decisions. Suppose we have two theories T_1 and T_2 that predict observations O and not-O respectively. Then an experiment is *crucial* with respect to T_1 and T_2 if it generates exactly one of the two observation statements O or not-O. Duhem's arguments show that in general, one cannot count on finding such an experiment or observation. In place of crucial observations, Duhem cites *le bon sens* (good sense), a non-logical faculty by means of which scientists supposedly decide such issues. Regarding the nature of this faculty, there is in principle nothing that rules out personal taste and cultural bias. That scientists prefer lofty appeals to *Occam's razor*, while mathematicians employ justificative terms like *beauty* and *elegance*, does not exclude less savory influences.

So much for Duhem; now what about Quine? The Quine thesis breaks down into two related theses. The first says that there is no distinction between analytic statements (e.g. definitions) and synthetic statements (e.g. empirical claims), and thus that the Duhem thesis applies equally to the so-called *a priori* disciplines. To make sense of this, we need to know the difference between *analytic* and *synthetic* statements. Analytic statements are supposed to be true by their meanings alone, matters of empirical fact notwithstanding, while synthetic statements amount to empirical facts themselves. Since analytic statements are necessarily true statements of the kind found in logic and mathematics, while synthetic statements are contingently true statements of the kind found in science, Quine's first thesis posits a kind of equivalence between mathematics and science. In particular, it says that epistemological claims about the sciences should apply to mathematics as well, and that Duhem's thesis should thus apply to both.

Quine's second thesis involves the concept of *reductionism*. Reductionism is the claim that statements about some subject can be reduced to, or fully explained in terms of, statements about some (usually more basic) subject. For example, to pursue chemical reductionism with respect to the mind is to claim that mental processes are really no more than biochemical interactions. Specifically, Quine breaks from Duhem in holding that not all theoretical claims, i.e. theories, can be reduced to observation statements. But then empirical observations "underdetermine" theories and cannot decide between them. This leads to a concept known as *Quine's holism*; because no observation can reveal which member(s) of a set of theoretical statements should be re-evaluated, the re-evaluation of some statements entails the re-evaluation of all.

Quine combined his two theses as follows. First, he noted that a reduction is essentially an analytic statement to the effect that one theory, e.g. a theory of mind, is defined on another theory, e.g. a theory of chemistry. Next, he noted that if there are no analytic statements, then reductions are impossible. From this, he concluded that his two theses were essentially identical. But although the resulting unified thesis resembled Duhem's, it differed in scope. For whereas Duhem had applied his own thesis only to physical theories, and perhaps only to theoretical hypothesis rather than theories with directly observable consequences, Quine applied his version to the entirety of human knowledge, including mathematics. If we sweep this rather important distinction under the rug, we get the so-called "Duhem–Quine thesis".

Because the Duhem–Quine thesis implies that scientific theories are underdetermined by physical evidence, it is sometimes called the *Underdetermination Thesis*. Specifically, it says that because the addition of new auxiliary hypotheses, e.g. conditionals involving "if ... then" statements, would enable each of two distinct theories on the same scientific or mathematical topic to accommodate any new piece of evidence, no physical observation could ever decide between them.

The messages of Duhem–Quine and Löwenheim–Skolem are as follows: universes do not uniquely determine theories according to empirical laws of scientific observation, and theories do not uniquely determine universes according to rational laws of mathematics. The model-theoretic correspondence between theories and their universes is subject to ambiguity in both directions. If we add this descriptive kind of ambiguity to ambiguities of measurement, e.g. the Heisenberg Uncertainty Principle that governs the subatomic scale of reality, and the internal theoretical ambiguity captured by undecidability, we see that ambiguity is an inescapable ingredient of our knowledge of the world. It seems that math and science are ... well, inexact sciences.

How, then, can we ever form a true picture of reality? There may be a way. For example, we could begin with the premise that such a picture exists, if only as a "limit" of theorization (ignoring for now the matter of showing that such a limit exists). Then we could educe categorical relationships involving the logical properties of this limit to arrive at a description of reality in terms of reality itself. In other words, we could build a self-referential theory of reality whose variables represent reality itself, and whose relationships are logical tautologies. Then we could add an instructive twist. Since logic consists of the rules of thought, i.e. of mind, what we would really be doing is interpreting reality in a generic theory of mind based on logic. By definition, the result would be a *cognitive-theoretic model of the universe*.

Gödel used the term *incompleteness* to describe that property of axiomatic systems due to which they contain undecidable statements. Essentially, he showed that all sufficiently powerful axiomatic systems are incomplete by showing that if they were not, they would be *inconsistent*. Saying that a theory is "inconsistent" amounts to saying that it contains one or more irresolvable paradoxes. Unfortunately, since any such paradox destroys the distinction between *true* and *false* with respect to the theory, the entire theory is crippled by the inclusion of a single one. This makes consistency a primary necessity in the construction of theories, giving it priority over proof and prediction. A cognitive-theoretic model of the universe would place scientific and mathematical reality in a self-consistent logical environment, there to await resolutions for its most intractable paradoxes.

For example, modern physics is bedeviled by paradoxes involving the origin and directionality of time, the collapse of the quantum wave function, quantum nonlocality, and the containment problem of cosmology. Were someone to present a simple, elegant theory resolving these paradoxes without sacrificing the benefits of existing theories, the resolutions would carry more weight than any number of predictions. Similarly, any theory and model conservatively resolving the self-inclusion paradoxes besetting the mathematical theory of sets, which underlies almost every other kind of mathematics, could demand acceptance on that basis alone. Wherever there is an intractable scientific or mathematical paradox, there is dire need of a theory and model to resolve it.

If such a theory and model exist – and for the sake of human knowledge, they had *better* exist – they use a logical metalanguage with sufficient expressive power to characterize and analyze the limitations of science and mathematics, and are therefore philosophical and metamathematical in nature. This is because no lower level of discourse is capable of uniting two disciplines that exclude each other's content as thoroughly as do science and mathematics.

Now here's the bottom line: such a theory and model do indeed exist. But for now, let us satisfy ourselves with having glimpsed the rainbow under which this theoretic pot of gold awaits us.

On Ayn Rand's Philosophy

The history of philosophy and culture is a grand, recursively-scaled dialectic. A person or school, a group or generation, espouses a thesis; the other side responds with its antithesis; the two extremes are then combined in a synthesis imbued with both perspectives. Ayn Rand can be best understood as a philosophical reactionary in this well-established tradition, the creator and champion of a dual antithesis directed against what she regarded as two devastating assaults on human individuality.The first of these assaults was religion; at the age of thirteen, she decided with certainty that she was an atheist. The second was communism, long the bane of her Russian homeland and still a geopolitical threat. Rand's dual antithesis consists of a mixture of atheism, materialism and extreme individualism, recast as "logic and objectivity" and aggressively presented as an affirmation of human freedom and self-interest. Critics sometimes dismiss this philosophy, called *objectivism*, as a mere capitalistic twist on communism, an over-simplistic and logically insupportable brand of egoism cloaked in empty protestations of rationality. Others point to the cult-like atmosphere of various Ayn Rand organizations and study groups; while such groups ostensibly exist to promote earnest philosophical consideration of Rand's writings, a few of them are reputed to enforce cult-like obedience to her every stated opinion, forbidding critical appraisal and discouraging exposure to alternative viewpoints. But even if these criticisms are factual, they should not dissuade us from looking for strands of truth in her message.

Many young people go through a phase during which they passionately embrace Rand's philosophy. The typical Rand hero or heroine, a physically attractive nonconformist driven by a combination of iconoclasm, creative innovation, intelligence, productivity, machinelike efficiency and competitive, take-no-prisoners self-interest, can be irresistible to one struggling against social adversity to define one's individuality. It matters not to such a reader that in a world consisting solely of Rand heroes and heroines, there would be neither enough wealth and power to reward them all for their brilliance nor enough individualistic elbow room to go around, forcing them to steamroller each other until the vast majority had been flattened into a seamless backdrop of mediocrity against which the peerless few could shine like stars. Nor does it matter that while such a mindset may be psychologically viable for one whose constructive *raison d'être* demands a radical departure from the beaten path, one of less than stellar ability would be more likely to find it a delayed prescription for self-disappointment. The thing to remember is that it fills a psychological need on the part of the reader, serving as a source of strength in a time of personal need.

The holes in Rand's philosophy are easy to find. For example, despite the demonstrable inadequacy of standard empirical arguments to decide the question of the existence of God, her theology (or lack thereof) is largely based on them. As another example, she maintains that personal selfishness and ambition are virtues and altruism is a vice, thereby effectively asserting that altruism, defined as an unselfish regard for the welfare of others, is inconsistent with individual self-interest. Since there are plausible scenarios in which the survival of the human race would depend on the self-sacrifice of one individual, this amounts to an assertion that letting the human race expire in order to ensure one's personal survival is virtuous, whereas saving the human race by means of self-sacrifice is corrupt. Bearing in mind that Rand's version of ethics displays very little resemblance to the norm, this seems muddled even by the light of her "man is an end in himself" dictum. In fact, there is a sense in which the conventional definitions of altruism and selfishness are semantically inconsistent or at least incomplete; because there are multiple levels of self, including collective levels, there are multiple "levels of selfishness" *including* altruism. But Rand, believing in the unconditional independence of the individual, would not have agreed with this. She would have found the idea that altruism is selfish, and true selfishness altruistic, quite unacceptable.

But it is true nonetheless. The human species has many levels of organization, with each of which is associated a measure of utility or value. The individual comprises only one of these levels. Using mathematical decision theory, it can be shown that there are many situations in which excessive self-interest on the part of the individual is at odds with the self-interest of the larger groups to which the individual belongs, ultimately including society as a whole, with implications relating directly back to the welfare of the individual. Two well-known examples are the Tragedy of the Commons, where the overutilization of common resources leads to economic disaster, and the Prisoner's Dilemma, a lesson in mutual cooperation and the value of loyalty. Equivalently, there are many levels of "self" with respect to utility, and they are not automatically in mutual accord. In the event of a global economic breakdown involving the highest level of Self, all lesser selves go down with the ship regardless of their putative "independence". It follows that denying or downplaying higher levels of self is neither logical nor objective. When it comes to rational decision theory and economics, it turns out that no man is an island after all.

Nevertheless, Rand's literary protagonists exhibit a stunningly naive approach to deontology, eschewing altruism and blithely assuming that individual self-interest is the only kind of self-interest worth acknowledging. To the eternal disgust of those with more ability than good fortune, real life produces an endless stream of cases in which people sporting this insufferable sort of attitude reap spectacular rewards while pressing what seems to be a cheater's thumb on the scale of destiny, riding to riches and power on a combination of ability, manipulation and outrageous good fortune shamelessly rendered as ability alone. But this is possible only where individual and social self-interest coincide, and even if one is egocentrically convinced that society can drop dead and bury its own remains with regard to any point of opposition, such coincidence cannot be taken for granted. And where it is absent, excessive pursuit of individual self-interest can cause the utility and wellbeing of individual and society alike to take a catastrophic nosedive. For this reason, enlightened individualists temper their ideological intransigence and trim their senses of entitlement in order to avoid contributing to a global economic catastrophe, continuing as best they can to live up to high standards of excellence, originality and personal integrity.

When an author's writings are powerful, appealing, and designed to illustrate a fundamental philosophical platform, it is all the more important to evaluate them fairly and objectively. When reading the work of Ayn Rand, we need not fear to be inspired by her single-minded vision of courageous individuality and creative self-actualization. After all, there are times and places in history and the everyday world which demand that the individual take a strong and independent stand. But this does not require that we dispense forever with empathy and compassion, even when the author acidly assures us that such sentiments are contemptible and counterproductive. As long as we remember that the individual is free to choose goals that are consistent with the interests of other individuals and society at large – as long as the individual is understood as a unique part of a greater whole in which resides a large part of the meaning of life – there can be little harm in a constructively motivated shot of pure selfishness every now and then provided, of course, that one resists the self-righteous temptation to chase it down with a shot of self-entitlement poured from a bottle obnoxiously labeled "Logic & Objectivity".

This futuristic novella, written in 1937, is one of Rand's earliest and most popular works. In it, she describes a terrifying world in which individuals have sacrificed their selfhood to the Collective. The word "I" has been abolished from the language and the great oppressive "We" reigns supreme ... until deep within the hive, one brave individual awakens from his forced slumber and embarks on a rebellious quest for forbidden knowledge. One cannot help but notice that by the utopian standards of modern PC (Political Correctness), this oppressive society is every bit the "promised land" that it claims to be. Right now, there are people on earth who dream that one day this kind of world will rise from the smoldering ashes of the one we now inhabit. Some of them even live in the United States. And in other places, their dream is all but a *fait accompli*.

In *Anthem*, Rand raises a burning question: what kind of world do most of us really want? At first glance, the answer seems simple: a world in which the individual and the collective have patched up their differences and learned to live in harmony. A world in which the rights and dignity of the individual are no longer at odds with collective levels of human selfhood, and in which the individual and the collective operate synergistically as parallel phases of human existence. A world in which the best parts of Rand's philosophy, those which powerfully affirm human dignity and freedom, can live happily with the indispensable invariants of collective utilitarianism. But is such a world realizable? With due allowance for the inevitable imperfections of democracy, the short answer is "yes". But since neither Rand nor her detractors have been able to define it for us, much less tell us how to bring it about, we find ourselves obliged to take renewed stock of the dialectic and seek a constructive synthesis. Fortunately, this task has been recognized and accepted, and thanks to the powers of human reason extolled by this brilliant author, the solution is already partially in hand.

Originally dismissed by critics, *Anthem* has sold over 2.5 million copies. The fact that it continues to sell at a rate of more than 60,000 copies per year is an unmistakable tribute to the power of Rand's message.

REFERENCES

Darwin, C. (1999) *On the Origin of Species*. New York: Bantam Classics. Original work published in 1859.

Descartes, R. (1996) *Descartes: Meditations on First Philosophy with Selections from the Objections and Replies*. Edited by J. Cottingham. Cambridge: Cambridge University Press.

Duhem, P. (1954) *The Aim and Structure of Physical Theory*. Translated by P. P. Wiener, foreword by L. de Broglie. New Jersey: Princeton University Press. Originally published under the title *La Théorie physique: Son objet, et sa structure*. Paris: Chevalier & Rivière, 1906.

Eldredge, N. & Gould S. J. (1972) Punctuated Equilibria: An Alternative to Phyiletic Gradualism. In Thomas J. M. Schopf (Ed.) *Models in Paleobiology*. San Francisco: Freeman Cooper & Company, pp. 82–115.

Fisher C. M. (2001) If There Were No Free Will. *Medical Hypotheses*, Vol. 56, Issue 3, pp. 364–366.

Gödel, K. (1962) *On Formally Undecidable Propositions of Principia Mathematica and Related Systems*. Translated by B. Meltzer. New York: Basic Books. Originally published under the title "Über formal unentscheidbare Sätze der Principia Mathematica und verwandter Systeme I" in *Monatshefte für Mathematik*, Vol. 38, Issue 1, December 1931.

Goodman N. (1955) *Fact, Fiction, and Forecast*. Cambridge, MA: Harvard University Press

Gould, S. J. (1989) *Wonderful Life: The Burgess Shale and the History of Nature*. New York: W. W. Norton & Company.

Hartle, J. B. & Hawking, S. W. (1983) Wave Function of the Universe. *Physical Review D*, Vol. 28, No. 12, 2960–75.

Hawking, S. W. (1988) *A Brief History of Time: From the Big Bang to Black Holes.* Introduction by C. Sagan, illustrated by R. Miller. New York: Bantam Books.

Hume, D. (1975) *Enquiries Concerning Human Understanding and Concerning the Principles of Morals.* 3rd Edition. Edited by L. A. Selby-Bigge & P. H. Nidditch. Oxford: Oxford University Press. Reprinted from the posthumous edition of 1777. Original work published in 1748 and 1751.

Kant, I. (1965) *The Critique of Pure Reason.* Translated by N. K. Smith. New York: St. Martin's Press. Original work published in 1781.

Langan, C. M. (1989) The Resolution of Newcomb's Paradox. *Noesis*, No. 44.

Langan, C. M. (2002) *The Cognitive-Theoretic Model of the Universe: A New Kind of Reality Theory.* Princeton, MO: Mega Foundation Press. Originally published in *Progress in Complexity, Information, and Design*, Double Issue, Vols. 1.2–3.

Levy S. (1997) The Brain's Last Stand. *Newsweek*, 05 May, pp. 50–56.

Libet B., Gleason C. A., Wright E. W., Pearl D. K. (1983) Time of Conscious Intention to Act in Relation to Onset of Cerebral Activity (Readiness-Potential): The Unconscious Initiation of a Freely Voluntary Act. *Brain*, Vol. 106, Issue 3, pp. 623–642.

Löwenheim, L. (1967) On Possibilities in the Calculus of Relatives. In Jean Van Heijenoort's *From Frege to Gödel: A Source Book in Mathematical Logic, 1879–1931*, pp. 228–251. Translated by S. Bauer-Mengelberg. Cambridge, MA: Harvard University Press. Originally published under the title "Über Möglichkeiten im Relativkalkül" in *Mathematische Annalen*, Vol. 76, Issue 4, pp. 447–470, December 1915.

Nozick, R. (1970) Newcomb's Problem and Two Principles of Choice. In N. Rescher (Ed.) *Essays in Honor of Carl G. Hempel: A Tribute on the Occasion of his Sixty-Fifth Birthday*, pp. 114–146. New York: Humanities Press.

REFERENCES

Rand, A. (1938) *Anthem*. London: Cassell & Co.

Reed L. (1974) *The Complete Limerick Book: The Origin, History, and Achievements of the Limerick, with about 350 selected examples.* Illustrated by H. M. Bateman. Detroit: Gale Research Company. Reprinted from the 1925 Jarrolds Publishers edition.

Quine, W. V. (1951) Two Dogmas of Empiricism. *The Philosophical Review*, Vol. 60, No. 1, pp. 20–43.

Skolem, T. (1967) Logico-combinatorial Investigations in the Satisfiability or Provability of Mathematical Propositions: A simplified Proof of a Theorem by L. Löwenheim and Generalizations of the Theorem. In Jean Van Heijenoort's *From Frege to Gödel: A Source Book in Mathematical Logic, 1879–1931*, pp. 252–263. Translated by S. Bauer-Mengelberg. Cambridge, MA: Harvard University Press. Originally published under the title "Logisch-kombinatorische Untersuchungen über die Erfüllbarkeit oder Beweisbarkeit mathematischer Sätze nebst einem Theoreme Über dichte Mengen" in *Skrifter utgit av Videnskapsselskapet i Kristiania 1920*, No. 4, pp. 1–36.

Wheeler, J. A. (1979) From the Big Bang to the Big Crunch. *Cosmic Search Magazine*, Vol. 1, Issue 4, pp. 2–8.

Wheeler, J. A. (1986) How Come the Quantum? *Annals of the New York Academy of Sciences*, Vol. 480, Issue 1: New Techniques and Ideas in Quantum Measurement Theory, pp. 304–316.

Wheeler, J. A. (1990a) Information, Physics, Quantum: The Search for Links. In W. H. Zurek (Ed.) *Complexity, Entropy and the Physics of Information, SFI Studies in the Sciences of Complexity*, Vol. VIII, pp. 3–28. Addison-Wesley Educational Publishing Company.

Wheeler, J. A. (1990b) *A Journey into Gravity and Spacetime*. New York: Scientific American Library.

Whitemore, H. (2015) *Breaking the Code*. London: Samuel French. First staged at Theatre Royal, London, 21 October 1986.

www.ingramcontent.com/pod-product-compliance
Lightning Source LLC
Chambersburg PA
CBHW021404090426
42742CB00009B/1001